CHRISTIAN LIFE & PRACTICE

Christian Life & Practice

ANGLICAN ESSAYS

OWEN C. THOMAS

CASCADE *Books* · Eugene, Oregon

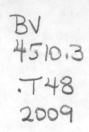
CHRISTIAN LIFE AND PRACTICE
Anglican Essays

Cascade Books
Division of Wipf and Stock Publishers
199 W. 8th Ave., Suite 3
Eugene, OR 97401

www.wipfandstock.com

ISBN 13: 978-1-55635-842-5

Cataloging-in-Publication data:

Thomas, Owen C.

    Christian life and practice : Anglican essays / Owen C. Thomas.

    xiv + 148 p. ; 23 cm.

    Includes bibliographic references and index.

    ISBN 13: 978-1-55635-842-5

    1. Theology. 2. Christianity—20th century. I. Title.

BR50 .T48 2008

Manufactured in the U.S.A.

To my former students and colleagues with gratitude.

TABLE OF CONTENTS

ACKNOWLEDGMENTS

I AM HAPPY TO acknowledge and thank the many people to whom I have been indebted over the years for inspiration, conversation, ideas, and criticism. They include my teachers, colleagues, and students at the Episcopal Divinity School, Weston School of Theology, the Gregorian University and the North American College in Rome, the Boston Theological Society, the New Haven Theological Group, the American Theological Society, the American Academy of Religion, the North American Paul Tillich Society, the Pacific Coast Theological Society, and the Graduate Theological Union. The number of individuals is too large to list here, but I must include a few who have helped me directly in the preparation of these essays: Harvey Guthrie, Professor Emeritus of the Episcopal Divinity School, Prof. Charles Hefling of Boston College, Prof. Arthur Holder of the Graduate Theological Union, and my wife, Dr. Margaret R. Miles of the Harvard Divinity School and the Graduate Theological Union, with whom conversations over the past thirty years on matters historical, theological, and existential have informed my thinking, writing, and life.

I am also indebted to the following publishers and journals for permission to publish the following essays:

Cowley Publications, A Member of The Rowman & Littlefield Publishing Group, for "The Story of Two Communities," in *Our Selves, Our Soul and Bodies*, edited by Charles Hefling. (Copyright Cowley Publications, 1996).

Sewanee Theological Review, published by The School of Theology of The University of the South, Sewanee, Tenessee, for "Parish Ministry: A Theologian's Perspective," *STR* 40:4 (1997) 444–56.

Anglican Theological Review, (© ATR ISSN 0003-3286) for "Some Problems in Contemporary Christian Spirituality," *ATR* 82:2 (2000) 267–81; "The Poverty of Preaching in the Episcopal Church," *ATR* 85:3 (2003) 429–45; and "Spiritual But Not Religious: The Influence of the Current Romantic Movement," *ATR* 88:4 (2006) 397–415.

INTRODUCTION

As the title indicates, this collection of essays treats the Christian life and practice from the point of view of the Anglican tradition. It may be helpful to the reader to know something about the author. I came to the Anglican tradition as an adult after being raised by atheist socialist parents who were disciples of John Dewey and his naturalistic humanist world view.[1] My first brief career was in physics with a college major and two years of graduate study in that field. Shortly before being drafted into the Navy in World War II, I was baptized by the Episcopal chaplain at Cornell University. I was sent to the Naval Research Laboratory in Washington DC where I engaged in research and development in ultra-high frequency radiation, namely, radar and counter measures. At the end of the war, I worked for a year as a lay assistant at St. John's Church, Lafayette Square, in Washington DC, with the Reverend James A. Pike, later Dean of the Cathedral of St. John the Divine in New York and Bishop of California, and the Reverend Howard A. Johnson, later Professor of Theology at the School of Theology of the University of the South, and a Kierkegaard expert, who were my first mentors in the Christian faith and life. At the end of that year I attended the Episcopal Theological School and Cambridge, MA, and then studied for a doctorate in the philosophy of religion at Columbia University and Union Theological Seminary. Since then I have taught theology and the philosophy of religion at the Episcopal Theological School (now Episcopal Divinity School) for over forty years, as well as at three other theological faculties.

1. For the details, see my chapter in Pike, *Modern Canterbury Pilgrims*. However, this is now, in an ecumenical age, a somewhat embarrassingly triumphalist book.

Given the subject matter of this book, I should explain that although I have never been the rector of a parish, I have always worked part-time in various parishes in the Dioceses of Massachusetts, New Hampshire, and California. I have also functioned as a pastoral counselor and spiritual director, trained in the latter discipline in a peer group at the monastery of the Society of St. John the Evangelist in Cambridge.

I decided to publish these essays because I had become aware of trends in the Episcopal Church, as well as other churches, in their theory and practice of the Christian life that concerned me, especially in regard to preaching, parish ministry, the emphasis on private life rather than public life, and the new phenomenon of spirituality. Thus, a majority of the essays in this volume are critical in character. In fact, as I look back over my various writings I can see that this critical approach has marked many of them. For example, I have been critical of the critique of religion by the secular theology of the 1960s, the concept of God as being itself, the emphasis on experience as the main criterion of theology, the plural- ist view of other religions, and the influence of the perennial philosophy, and so forth.[2] I believe that my critical approach is not simply negative but is also constructive and aimed at reform.

After the first chapter in which an overview of an Anglican inter- pretation of Christian life and practice is outlined, the next two chapters focus on what I have called the spirituality movement. It arose in the 1970s and has now become a vast multimillion dollar industry involv- ing thousands of new full-time specialists, many new centers of spiritual formation, a great many new professorial chairs in seminaries and other graduate schools, a large new area of publishing that produces hundreds of new books on spirituality every year, the creation of new sections on spirituality in all bookstores, and the introduction of spirituality into every other area of cultural and economic life. Needless to say, this move- ment has had a major impact on American and British churches. In the second chapter, I discuss what I believe to be the many confusions and misunderstandings in this movement and suggest ways to overcome them. In the third chapter, I propose an explanation for the sudden emergence, widespread influence, and cultural power of this movement, which I believe to be a new Romantic movement in U.S. and British cul-

2. See Thomas, *What Is It That Theologians Do*.

ture similar to the first Romantic movement of the late eighteenth and early nineteenth centuries.

In the fourth chapter, I offer a critique of parish ministry as I see it practiced in churches today. In its original form this was a lecture I gave regularly in a course on parish ministry at the Episcopal Divinity School conducted by the late Reverend Dr. George Hunter. This critique is based on an interpretation of the mission of the church to the public world of politics and economics, as well as to the private life of the family. I suggest that the residential parish is in the worst possible position for carrying out the mission of the church to public life and I suggest what might be done to overcome this. I realize that the emphasis on the public life of politics and economics is a recurring theme in these essays, and I attribute this to the influence of my parents who were deeply involved in and committed to public life. My mother's uncle was Herbert Croly, founder of *The New Republic* and mentor to the leaders of the Progressive movement, including Theodore Roosevelt and Woodrow Wilson, through his books *The Promise of American Life* (1909) and *Progressive Democracy* (1914). My mother was a protégé of the suffragists, worked at The Bureau for Municipal Research, a Progessive era good government organization in New York City, and was an expert in foreign affairs and international relations as director of the League of Nations Association, later the United Nations Association. My father was a PhD in political science, and worked in city, state, and national politics, and as an organizer, teacher, and author. The result of this influence was that I campaigned passionately for Al Smith for President in 1928 at a tender age, was elected on the presidential primary ballot to the Cambridge Democratic City Committee for twenty-five years, and served as an associate member of the Alameda County Democratic Central Committee in California for a few years.

The fifth chapter is a fictional piece originally presented to a clergy group in the Diocese of Massachusetts in 1969. It recounts the experience of the new rector of a parish in which the church, parish house, and rectory have been completely destroyed in a fire. It treats the responsibility of the church for the public life of its members, and also the inordinate amount of the churches' financial and human resources devoted to buildings and grounds. The sixth chapter deals with the widespread consensus that preaching in the Episcopal Church is generally poor, suggests that the source of this lies in the failure of the seminaries to treat the theology of preaching, and points a way to the improvement of preaching. Chapter

7 offers an outline of the place and character of prayer in the Anglican tradition with an emphasis on honesty in prayer and on the centrality of petitionary prayer. It also discusses the relation of this view of prayer to the new emphasis on contemplative prayer growing out of the current spirituality and Romantic movements.

Chapter 8 deals with the crisis in the Episcopal Church and the Anglican Communion over the ordination of a non-celibate homosexual priest as Bishop of New Hampshire. It is an essay taken from a book on this subject that was published in 1996, and it describes how two communities dealt with the appearance of openly homosexual people in their midst, namely, the Episcopal Divinity School in Cambridge, MA, and the Church of St. John the Evangelist in Boston. I conclude that a major factor in the decisions of these two communities to open themselves to the full inclusion of non-celibate homosexual people has been their experience of living with them in a church community, getting to know them as friends, and working together with them in the mission of the church. Furthermore, I suggest that any judgment on this issue apart from this kind of knowledge and experience should be seriously questioned. An Appendix to this chapter treats what I call the hysteria over homosexuality and finds the origins of it in the literal interpretation of the purity codes in Leviticus through the influence of Puritanism and Pietism in American, African, and Southeast Asian churches.

The final chapter in the book is a meditation on the implications of biblical prophecy for our view of politics today, especially in relation to what can be called the social health of the nation. It was originally a sermon that I preached at St. Mark's Church in Berkeley shortly before the presidential election in 2000. This chapter concludes with an Appendix on the misleading character of the mentality of activist, movement, and third party politics, which has led to the eight years of the Bush administration.

CHAPTER ONE

An Anglican Interpretation of the Christian Life[1]

THE CHRISTIAN LIFE IS our life of faith and discipleship before God in the church and the world. It is our whole life in the presence of God as members of the church and participants in its life, and as members of a family, a place of employment, town, city, state, nation, world, and natural universe. This definition, of course, involves theologically normative judgments about sin, grace, and progress based on the authorities accepted in Anglicanism, namely, Scripture, tradition, reason, and experience. For those who have grown up in Christian households, entering upon the Christian life may be largely a matter of growing awareness. For others this will be a matter of a decision to depart one worldview, religious tradition, or denomination, and to enter another, that is, a conversion. This may be sudden, as in the case of Paul and Augustine, or it may be gradual. It may also be a continuing process in the Christian life of deepening one's conversion intellectually, morally, and emotionally.[2] Any kind of conversion can be a shaking, even devastating, experience, since conversion involves risk and a fundamental change of life, the dismantling of an old way of life and the beginning and growth in a new way.[3] Conversion is probably more a possibility today, at least in the United States, than it

1. This topic is almost universally referred to today as "spirituality." I believe, however, that the usage of the term in the current spirituality movement is misleading in many ways. See chapter 2.

2. See Allen, *Spiritual Theology*, ch. 3.

3. See Crossman, *The God that Failed*.

1

was in the first half of the last century. Robert Wuthnow has argued that we have moved from a spirituality of dwelling to one of seeking. He states that "a traditional spirituality of inhabiting sacred places [which emphasizes habitation] has given way to a new spirituality of seeking [which emphasizes negotiation]."[4]

There have been many interpretations of the Christian life in this sense from the very beginning. For example, in the first century, there were distinct interpretations in Jewish Christian and Gentile Christian communities, in communities associated with Johannine and Pauline interpretations of the Gospel, and in communities associated with one of the Synoptic traditions. Later, different interpretations developed in monastic communities, in Eastern and Western Christianity, in Roman Catholic and Protestant traditions, and in variations of these in the different cultures of the world.

One way of distinguishing these different interpretations of the Christian life is to note that that they are based on different understandings of what constitutes membership in the church. One type is confessional. Here what constitutes membership is confessing the faith of the church as represented in its creeds and doctrines. A second type is experiential. What makes you a member of a church is having had a particular kind of experience, for example, an experience of conversion or of receiving the gifts of the Spirit. A third type is pragmatic. What makes you a member of a church is your practice, your participation in the practices of the church, doing what the church does.[5]

Anglicanism generally does not focus on a confession of faith, although this is included in the service of baptism and in the recital of the creed at the Eucharist. Also, the Book of Common Prayer includes a confession of faith deriving from the sixteenth century, namely, the Articles of Religion. The Articles, however, are much briefer than the other Protestant and Roman Catholic confessions of that period, are more general and less detailed than the others, and have not been used as a detailed test of orthodoxy in the past century as the others have.[6]

4. Wuthnow, After Heaven, 3f.

5. In this chapter I am indebted to my former colleagues at the Episcopal Divinity School in their book Wolf, Anglican Spirituality, and in this paragraph especially to Harvey Guthrie.

6. All ordinands in the Episcopal Church are required to sign a Declaration that they believe that the Bible is the Word of God and contains all things necessary to salva-

Also Anglicanism does not emphasize a particular kind of experience. Anglicanism does, however, focus on practice, on doing what the church does, as outlined in the *Book of Common Prayer*. Paul Elmer Moore and Frank Cross state that the "guiding principle of the Anglican *via media* . . . the single term to denote the ultimate law of Anglicanism [is] pragmatism . . . the genius of Anglicanism [can be described] as supremely pragmatic."[7] In this, Anglicanism follows the practice of rabbinic Judaism, the primitive church, and Eastern Orthodoxy.[8] A classic example of this in the Episcopal Church is found in the report of the Advisory Committee regarding the censure of the Right Reverend James A. Pike in 1967 when he was charged with heresy. The House of Bishops stated that the Report "establishes a position which we welcome and generally share." The Report states,

> When Episcopalians are questioned about the supposed orthodoxy or heterodoxy of one of their number, their most likely response is to ask whether or not he wishes—sincerely and responsibly—to join them in the celebration of God's being and goodness in the prayers and worship of the *Prayer Book*. Assuming his integrity, they would not be likely to press the question beyond that point. . . . We would say that the willingness of a person to share in the worship of the *Prayer Book* with a consenting mind is, for most purposes, an adequate test of his right to claim the privileges of the community.[9]

This approach has been put in a different way in the statement about doctrine that what is required in essentials is unity, in non-essentials, liberality, and in all things charity. Needless to say, there will always be a debate about what the essentials are and about the range of acceptable in-

---

tion and that they will conform to the doctrine, discipline, and worship of the Episcopal Church. The Articles are not mentioned. A similar declaration is required in the Church of England and in most of the other Provinces of the Anglican Communion. For the details, see Sykes, *Study of Anglicanism*, 140–42.

7. Moore and Cross, *Anglicanism: The Thought and Practice of the Church of England*, xxxii–iii.

8. See the references to the unpublished papers by David Novak and George Lindbeck, and to Lindbeck's book *The Nature of Doctrine*, in Thomas, *What Is It That Theologians Do*, 80–81.

9. Bayne, *Theological Freedom and Social Responsibility*, 21. Needless to say, there are those in the Episcopal Church today who would not subscribe to this view, but I believe that it is essential to Anglicanism.

terpretation of them. Rowan Williams has stated that Anglican theology is "pragmatic to the extent that [Anglicans] sought to answer the question, 'What should I do and say as someone brought into the community of Christ's faithful people?' For them, thinking about God was closely bound up with thinking about how human beings become holy, come to show in their lives the grace and glory of God."[10]

Needless to say, none of the major Christian traditions has been uniform in its interpretation of the Christian life. Within Anglicanism there have been three main interpretations of the Christian life: Evangelical, Latitudinarian or Broad Church, and Tractarian or Anglo-Catholic. The Evangelical interpretation of the Christian life has been a current in Anglicanism from the beginning. It was manifest in the late sixteenth century in the "prophesyings" in meetings of clergy and laity devoted to Bible study and prayer. In the same period the evangelical influence of Puritanism was seen in the "classis" system of committees of local presbyters who selected candidates for ordination, criticized sermons, and insisted on *ex tempore* prayer in public worship. In the eighteenth century the evangelical movement was led by Charles and John Wesley and later by Charles Simeon, vicar of Holy Trinity Church, Cambridge.[11] This interpretation of the Christian life emphasized the centrality of the word in Scripture (but was suspicious of the new historical-critical approach to scripture), preaching, personal testimony, the necessity of conversion in response to the cross of Christ, private and family prayer, world mission, philanthropy, social reform, and suspicion of Rome.[12]

The Latitudinarian or Broad Church interpretation began to emerge in the seventeenth century as a school of liberal, reasonable scholars and clergy who were weary of controversy and intensity of religious feeling, favored toleration of religious differences, and a life dedicated to the pursuit of goodness and righteousness. This tradition came to a full expression in the work of F. D. Maurice, founder of the Christian Socialist movement. His interpretation of the Christian life was based on an insight that the foundation of human nature was the righteousness of Christ, that Christ was the head of every person, whether acknowledged

10. "General Introduction," in Rowell, *Love's Redeeming Work*, xx.

11. In regard to John Wesley's status as an Anglican, he stated in 1790, "I declare once more that I live and die a member of the Church of England, and none that regard my judgment or advice will ever separate from it." Wesley, *Works of John Wesley*, 1:10.

12. See Wakefield, "Anglican Spirituality," 275.

or not. Therefore, all people are members of a species whose fundamental law is revealed in Christ to be what he called the law of sacrifice, rather than selfishness. To acknowledge this is to become fully human and a member of the church where this is expressed in prayer and corporate worship.[13] After Maurice's death in 1872, the Broad Church movement was taken up by the Modern Churchmen's Union that promoted liberal religious thought, doctrinal restatement, and liturgical revision, all in line with modern research.

The Tractarian or Anglo-Catholic interpretation of the Christian life arose in the Oxford Movement and the publication of "Tracts for The Times" written by Newman, Pusey, Keble, and others in the 1830s. It was a movement to recover the catholicity of Anglicanism, to oppose its subordination to the state, to counter evangelicalism as relying too much on individual experience, and also to oppose the liberalism represented by the new German biblical scholarship. It sought the origins and criterion of Anglicanism not in the Reformation but rather in the fathers and councils of the early church. It was a holiness movement that sought sanctification through the disciplines of fasting and penance and participation in the sacraments, especially the Eucharist. [14]

Anglo-Catholics, however, have been divided since the nineteenth century over the issue of "ritualism," namely, the ceremonial accompanying the Eucharist.[15] "The most damaging of the divisions among Anglo-Catholics was that over whether to base their ceremonial additions to the prayer book liturgy on medieval English or Modern Roman Catholic examples."[16] The former stance was held by the Alcuin Club and by Percy Dearmer in his book *The Parson's Handbook*, which focused on the use of the Diocese of Salisbury (Sarum) and the Ornaments Rubric of 1662. The latter stance was maintained by the Society of St. Peter and St. Paul, which aimed at promoting the ceremonial of continental Roman Catholics.

Ideally, all these movements, however, are generally united in affirming the catholic, protestant, and liberal character of Anglicanism: catholic in affirming the catholic faith, order, and practice of the early church based on the Bible and outlined in the creeds and the first four

---

13. See Booty in Wolf, *Anglican Spirituality*, 81–82.
14. See Wakefield, "Anglican Spirituality," 277–82.
15. See Yates, *Anglican Ritualism*.
16. Ibid., 336.

ecumenical councils, without addition or subtraction; protestant in affirming priority of the Bible as the first norm of doctrine and as the way to keep the church *semper reformanda*, always being reformed; and liberal in the sense of openness to other Christian traditions and to the critical disciplines of the modern world. They are also united in affirming the communal, liturgical, sacramental, and pragmatic character of the Anglican interpretation of the Christian life. The focus is communal or corporate rather than individual, as distinct from what is probably the majority view in western Christianity in the modern period with its emphasis on individual devotion and meditation, and which is exacerbated by the individualism of contemporary U. S. society.[17] It is based on "common prayer" in public worship according to the *Book of Common Prayer*, which belongs not just to the clergy but also to all members. Thus it is also an interpretation of the Christian life that is liturgical in character—centered in corporate worship uniting word and sacrament—rather than in individual devotion or private prayer. In the same way, it is sacramentally focused on the Gospel sacraments of baptism, enacting entrance into the community and the conferring of grace, and Eucharist, enacting continued participation in the presence of God in Christ, plus the "Other Sacramental Rites" of confirmation, ordination, marriage, penance, and unction.[18] Anglicanism has always affirmed a balanced unity of word and sacrament, although it has usually been stronger on the sacraments than on the word.[19] The Anglican interpretation of the Christian life is practical or pragmatic is the sense noted above. What guides practice is a rule, and the rule is the *Book of Common Prayer*, which stands in the tradition of the Rule of St. Benedict.

The first Anglican prayer books were prepared by Thomas Cranmer in 1549 and 1552, and he drew on a variety of sources: the Latin rites, especially that of the Diocese of Salisbury, Cardinal Quiñones reform of the Latin Breviary, Lutheran experiments in liturgical reform, Greek liturgies, and the Spanish mozarabic rite.[20] Wakefield states,

> Anglican spirituality takes its character from the Book of Common Prayer. It is not essentially *mystical*. . . . The Book con-

17. See Bellah, *Habits of the Heart*.
18. See *Book of Common Prayer*, 860–61.
19. See chapter 6.
20. See Shepherd, *Oxford American Prayer Book Commentary*, xvi–xvii.

tains the seeds of that moralism which is so vital a part of classic
Anglicanism, which for a while in the eighteenth century took
over and is inseparable from the Caroline and Tractarian longing
for holiness. The aim of the Prayer Book is "a godly, righteous,
and sober life." It does not encourage flights into the spiritual
empyrean, and its *terminus ad quem* may be said to be "never
further than the cross." For some it may be the starting point of "a
devotion of rapture," but not for most; it does not encourage enthusiasm nor the perfectionism which was so much a part of the
Christianity of the radicals of 1640–1660 and of John Wesley. . . .
It became for many lay people a much-thumbed possession, not
simply to be taken down from the church rack on Sundays, but a
daily companion in the home, a manual of guidance meditation,
family devotions and inspiration for living.[21]

A. M. Allchin puts it this way:

It was the genius of Cranmer to bring together into a single volume many different things: the texts necessary for the Sunday
Eucharist, the texts for the daily office, the services for ordination,
the occasional offices which accompany the believer from birth
to burial. Thus there was, in the hands of any churchman who
could read, a book which linked private with public prayer, which
showed the Bible as text to be used in worship and which em-
braced the whole range of human life, personal as well as social.
It represented a balanced and inclusive vision of Christian prayer
and worship.[22]

The *Books of Common Prayer* of the sixteenth and seventeenth
centuries, along with the Authorized or King James version of the Bible
(1611), had a major impact on the language, literature, and music of the
English-speaking world. This appeared in the poetry of John Donne,
George Herbert, and Henry Vaughan of the seventeenth century and that
of T. S. Eliot, W. H. Auden, and R. S. Thomas in the twentieth. It also appeared in the libretto of Handel's *Messiah* in which the biblical passages
followed the lectionary of the *Prayer Book*. It appeared in the works of the
Inklings, a group of Anglican scholars at Oxford including the novels of
Charles Williams, J. R. R. Tolkien, and C. S. Lewis. As for music, Richard
Hooker, the leading Anglican theologian of the seventeenth century,

21. Wakefield, "Anglican Spirituality," 263.

22. A. M. Allchin, "Anglican Spirituality," in Sykes and Booty, *Study of Anglicanism*,
315.

praised its power to elevate the mind. Allchin, quoting Olivier Loyer, describes Hooker's view: "More than the other arts, [music] has this faculty to integrate contemplative reason and sensory perception; it is harmony and proportion, it speaks to the highest part of the soul, evoking the divine perception; but first of all it speaks to man's inferior faculties and makes use of their power."[23] Allchin summarizes all of the above:

> This is a tradition which by its form as well as by its content seems to speak of a particular perception of the link between grace and nature, faith and culture, divine and human, which has been characteristic of Anglican spirituality as a whole, and has had its influence more widely in the intellectual history of the English-speaking world. . . . There is something here which seems to activate and transform the human imagination.[24]

The interpretation of the Christian life in every Christian tradition is based on a rule of life, either explicit or implicit. We see the beginning of this in Acts 2:42: "They devoted themselves to the apostles' teaching and fellowship, to the breaking of bread and the prayers." The earliest explicit rules were those of the first monastic communities, and every Christian tradition developed its own rule as a guide for the Christian life. In the *Book of Common Prayer* (1979), a summary version of the rule is given in the Catechism: "The Duty of all Christians is to follow Christ; to come together week by week for corporate worship; and to work, pray, and give for the spread of the kingdom of God." Another version runs as follows: "The ministry of lay persons is to represent Christ and his Church; to bear witness to him wherever they may be; and, according to the gifts given to them, to carry on Christ's work of reconciliation in the world; and to take their place in the life, worship, and governance of the Church."[25] The rule is spelled out in detail in the *Prayer Book*.

An Anglican rule of life usually contains five points: (1) weekly public corporate worship with your community, normally the Sunday Eucharist; (2) daily private or family prayer, usually Morning or Evening Prayer or parts thereof as suggested in "Daily Devotions for Individuals and Families"[26] This should include at least the Lord's Prayer, the collect

23. Ibid., 320.
24. Ibid., 316, 318.
25. See *Book of Common Prayer*, 856, 855.
26. Ibid., 136–40

for the day, one of the Scripture readings from the lectionary, prayer for family, parish, community, the nation, and the world, free mental prayer about what is most urgent in one's life, and a brief meditation on one of the verses of Scripture;[27] (3) participation in the mission of the church in the parish and community understood as assisting in at least one of the functions of the parish, service of those in need in the community, testimony to God in Christ in word and deed for justice and peace; (4) appropriation of the tradition, often called spiritual reading, daily or at least weekly;[28] (5) and self-examination, at least weekly in preparation for the Eucharist, using one of the Penitential Orders in the *Prayer Book* (319, 351) or in spiritual direction.[29] The most important thing about a rule (*regula*) is regularity, what one can do regularly without strain. If you cannot manage it regularly without strain, then it should be revised or it will probably be useless or worse, guilt-producing.

Now what is the purpose of such a rule? It is an outline of the necessary bases of an Anglican version of the Christian life. Its purpose is to promote progress in the Christian life in the individual and the community. Progress in the Christian life has been formulated in many ways in Christian history. The traditional version is progress in the three stages of purgation, illumination, and union with God.[30] Other versions have included progress toward full participation in the reign of God; growing in communion with God through Christ by the Spirit; being conformed to the image of God in Christ by the Spirit; growing in holiness or sanctity; growing in grace toward the fullness of the Christian virtues of faith, hope, love, joy, and peace, and the greatest of these is love, love of God and love of neighbor. Love of God is interpreted in the Catechism in terms of the first four commandments of the Decalogue, and love of neighbor in the latter six commandments. Love of neighbor can be interpreted as whole-hearted concern for the well-being of any person whose life we

27. For a method of meditation on scripture passages, see Smith, *The Word Is Very Near You*; see also chapter 7 below for a further discussion of the various forms of prayer.

28. An ideal example of this is Martin L. Smith's book of daily meditations for Lent, *A Season for the Spirit*; there are many other sources both classical, as in Augustine's *Confessions*, and Jeremy Taylor's *Rule and Exercises of Holy Living*, and *Rule and Exercises of Holy Dying*, and also contemporary sources.

29. Assistance in working out a rule can be found in Society of St. John the Evangelist, *Rule of the Society of Saint John the Evangelist*.

30. See, for example, Thornton, *English Spirituality*, 16–20

can affect by our actions both in private and family life and our public life in work and citizenship.

Because of the situation of the United States in the world today, our actions in public life, especially electoral politics, affect the lives of every person in our community, state, nation, and the world. Therefore Christian formation or instruction for new members must include instruction in our access to electoral politics.[31] The involvement of the church and its members in public economic and political life has always been an important element in the Anglican understanding of the Christian life deriving in part from the (otherwise dubious) establishment of the Church of England.[32]

Growth or progress in the Christian life in Anglicanism can occasionally be aided and promoted by spiritual direction. Spiritual direction has been fairly common in all Christian churches but usually not by that name except in the Roman Catholic and Orthodox traditions. In the last four decades, however, that name has become universal in most traditions as a result of the spirituality movement.[33] Spiritual direction is the focusing of something that has been common in all churches, namely, the practice of Christians helping one another in the Christian life in their interactions in the Christian community. This is based on the gospel claim that God has come among us in Christ through the Spirit as our servant (*diakonos*, see Matt 20:28, Mark 10:45) and carries out a ministry (*diakonia*) to us through the creation, human society, and the church in all its functions: corporate worship, preaching, teaching, the liturgical year, pastoral care, special groups, and so forth. This ministry of God is mediated to us through our friends in the Christian community, and when this ministry is focused through the ministry of one person, it is called spiritual direction. Thus, there is a sense in which all members of the church give and receive spiritual direction most of the time. It is essentially being a Christian friend to a fellow pilgrim, helping a person to be fully ministered to by God through the church and the world.

The word "spiritual" can be misleading in that it may imply that spiritual direction deals only with one's prayer life. Direction, however, should deal with your whole life before God including your family life,

31. See chapter 9.

32. See Temple, *Christianity and Social Order*, and Booty's treatment of Temple in Wolf, *Anglican Spirituality*, 69–72.

33. See chapter 2.

your life as a worker, a citizen, and an aesthetic being as well as a moral and religious being, all in relation to God.[34] Also the word "direction" can be misleading in that it may imply an authoritarian relation. "Guidance" would be a better term, and in any case it is always mutual to some extent. There is, however, another pole in the spectrum of spiritual direction, namely, the one emphasizing authority, hierarchy, and detachment. An element of truth in this pole is that a proper detachment can be an important factor in assessing a person's spiritual situation, and that an intimate friend is usually not the best person to be your spiritual director.

Spiritual direction is based on an ascetical theology, the study of the exercise, practice, or discipline of the Christian life. Traditional ascetical theology needs to be constantly reformed by the latest scriptural and historical studies and by reference to contemporary theories of psychological and faith development. Then it may be understood primarily not as the ladder of ascent or the way or journey to God but rather as the way *with* God on the basis of the way from God to us in Christ. Also, spiritual direction is often distinguished from penance, pastoral counseling, and formation or instruction in the Christian life. In my experience, however, spiritual direction occasionally moves into these areas and back again and does so appropriately.

Finally, there are certain dangers associated with the increasing interest in and demand for spiritual direction. They can be listed as individualism, privatism, clericalism, elitism, quietism, guruism, sexism, and what might be called schlock spirituality. Spiritual direction has sometimes tended to focus on the individual without reference to the life of the community, to focus on the private life of the individual apart from family, work, and public life, to focus on the problems of seminarians and clergy, to develop an inner circle of the elect or truly spiritual who are affluent enough to have the leisure for spiritual direction, retreats, and spiritual reading, to imply that the Christian life is not inevitably involved in the problems of the world, to cause directees to be enthralled by and to idolize their spiritual directors, to reinforce rather than to challenge the influences of our patriarchal society, and to be seduced by the banalities of New Age pop psychology.[35]

34. A clarification of the meaning of "spiritual" is offered in chapter 2.

35. See Rowthorn, *Liberation of the Laity*, 54–56.

The literature of the Anglican interpretation of the Christian life is vast. Classic examples are found in John Donne's *Devotions on Emergent Occasions* (1624), Lancelot Andrewes' *Preces Privatae* (1648), Jeremy Taylor's *The Rule and Exercises of Holy Living* (1650) and *The Rule and Exercises of Holy Dying* (1651), and in George Herbert's *A Priest to the Temple or The Country Parson* (1652). Among contemporary interpretations I am partial to *Anglican Spirituality*, edited by William J. Wolf, which stands in the Latitudinarian or Broad Church tradition of Anglicanism. This tradition was exemplified originally in the volume *Essays and Reviews*, which was published in 1860, the year after the publication of Darwin's *The Origin of Species*, and produced a storm of controversy. This tradition aims to be open to all the critical disciplines of the modern world including philosophy, the natural and human sciences, and especially historical criticism. In regard to the Christian life, this includes openness to illumination from other Christian traditions and other religious traditions, as well as from secular traditions.[36]

One issue that divides Anglicans in their understanding of the Christian life is whether or not to accept or reject the influence of the Platonist tradition. By the latter I am referring to that philosophical tradition that began with Plato, was continued in Aristotle, in the Middle Platonists of the second century, in the so-called Neoplatonism of Plotinus and his followers of the third to the fifth centuries, and in the revival of this tradition at the Renaissance.[37] For example, the influence of this tradition appears in the differences between Evangelical and Anglo-Catholic interpretations. Platonism has been influential in the Christian tradition and the interpretation of the Christian life from the beginning; first in the Johannine tradition as distinct from the Pauline, then in those influenced by Middle Platonism such as Justin Martyr and Clement of Alexandria, those influenced by Neoplatonism including Augustine, Dionysius, and many others, in various theologians of the sixteenth century, and in those influenced by the idealist philosophers of the nineteenth century. There was some resistance to the Platonist tradition among the Reformers of the

36. I should note, however, that although I taught for many years at a seminary of the Broad Church tradition, I have felt at home theologically in a combination of the Broad Church and evangelical traditions, and liturgically in that version of the Anglo-Catholic tradition which is derived from medieval English usage rather than that of nineteenth-century Roman Catholicism.

37. See Drees, "Platonism and the Platonic Tradition."

sixteenth century, especially Luther, and in the work of Kierkegaard in the nineteenth century. In Anglicanism the influence of Platonism began in the work of the Renaissance scholars John Colet, Thomas More, and John Fisher. It was revived among the Cambridge Platonists of the seventeenth century, Benjamin Whichcote, Ralph Cudworth, John Smith, Henry More, and Nathaniel Culverwel. It reached a pinnacle in the last century in the work of William Ralph Inge, Dean of St. Paul's, who described himself as a disciple of Plotinus and stated, "We cannot preserve Platonism without Christianity, or Christianity without Platonism, or civilization without both."[38] Inge also pioneered the revived study of mysticism.

The positive attitude toward Platonism in Anglicanism is clearly the majority view. A major reason for this in the past half century is the current Romantic movement, which emerged in the 1960s and that, like its predecessor in the late eighteenth and early nineteenth centuries, is based in large measure on Neoplatonism and similar traditions.[39] There are, however, exceptions to this positive attitude, especially among evangelicals, whose emphasis is on the Bible, the cross of Christ, conversion, and evangelism. Evangelicals do not so much attack Platonism as simply ignore it. For example, in the book *Christian Spirituality* by a leading British evangelical Anglican theologian, Alister E. McGrath, there are brief references to the influence of Platonism on Gregory of Nyssa and Augustine but nothing else. On the other hand, there is W. H. V. Reade, Tutor in philosophy at Oxford and Dean of Keble College in the last century, who, in his book *The Christian Challenge to Philosophy*, attacks Platonism in two chapters entitled "The Christian Rejection of Platonism," treating history, faith, monotheism, creation, and the body. He states, "'Christian Platonism,' if we propose to take the expression seriously, is nothing less than a contradiction in terms. . . . The discrepancies between Christianity and Platonism, when we get down to first principles, are so radical that only by complete misunderstanding or willful blindness is it possible to profess allegiance to both."[40] A positive response to Reade's book can be found in the review by Norman Pittenger, a leading American Anglican

38. Inge, *Philosophy of Plotinus*, 2:227.

39. See Thomas, "On Doing Theology During a Romantic Movement," in Thomas, *What Is It That Theologians Do*, ch. 5. For surveys of this tradition, see Inge, *Platonic Tradition in English Religious Thought*; Muirhead, *Platonic Tradition in Anglo-Saxon Philosophy*; and Cassirer, *Platonic Renaissance in England*.

40. Reade, *Christian Challenge to Philosophy*, 55.

theologian of the last century. He describes the book as "brilliant," "excellent," "learned," and "fascinating."[41]

Other Anglicans, including myself, have been influenced by Paul Ricoeur's view of the Platonist tradition, which is elaborated in his analysis of the four great myths of the origin of evil, among them the Adamic, or biblical myth, and the myth of the Exiled Soul, or the Platonist myth. Ricoeur states that these latter two myths are "radically heterogeneous" but that in Christian history the Platonist myth has often "contaminated" the biblical myth. Ricoeur concludes as follows:

> In its ascetic form as well in its mystical form, Platonizing Christianity adopts the opposition between contemplation and concupiscence, which, in its turn, introduces the opposition between the spiritual soul and the mortal and raving body; the old fear of defilement and the old fear of the body and sexuality are taken over by the new wisdom. . . . Thus there will be assembled, within the Christian experience, the conditions for a fusion with Neoplatonist spirituality, the remote heir of the myth of the exiled soul and the body-prison.[42]

How does this disagreement about Platonism affect the interpretation of the Christian life? Those who affirm a positive attitude toward Platonism will tend to stress the centrality of mysticism, the Christian life as a ladder of ascent toward God, and the centrality of contemplative prayer. "For the Platonists, the whole of human life should be prayer, since communion with God is the goal of everything."[43] They will also emphasize the priority of worship over service,[44] the tendency toward suppression of the bodily and psychic, the interpretation of salvation as *theosis* or deification, the incarnation rather than the atonement, and the sacraments rather than the word. An example of the latter can be found in John Henry Newman who, when commenting on the awakened and

41. See *The Anglican Theological Review* 9:2 (1952) 135, 137; see also Edmond Lab. Cherbonnier, "Is There a Biblical Metaphysic?" *Theology Today* 15:4 (1959) 454–69, which makes extensive use of Reade's book.

42. Ricoeur, *Symbolism of Evil*, 281, 335. The last phrase is a reference to passages in which Plato refers to the body as the prison or tomb of the soul. See *Phaedo* 81–83, *Cratylus* 400c, *Phaedrus* 250c, and *Gorgias* 493c.

43. Wakefield, *Christian Spirituality*, 270; see Thomas, *Introduction to Theology*, 294–300.

44. See Kirk, *Vision of God*, 441–51.

anxious sinner who goes to hear dissenting preachers, stated, "Had he been taught as a child, that the Sacraments, not preaching, are the sources of divine grace . . . we would not have so many wanderers from our fold, nor so many cold hearts within it."[45] Those who hold a negative attitude toward the Platonist tradition will tend to be critical of monistic mysticism[46] and to emphasize the experience of God mediated by the Bible in corporate worship, to stress the coming of God to us in the incarnation and the gift of the Spirit, and the primary importance of corporate prayer for the church and the world, and of service to those in need.

Does the rejection of the influence of the Platonist tradition mean the rejection of the influence of any philosophy, as some biblicists claim, or does it mean the affirmation of an alternate philosophical tradition, as others argue? This latter claim has been made by existentialist theologians, such as Bultmann and Gogarten, and by process theologians such as Hartshorne and Cobb. A third possibility, namely, the elaboration of a biblical metaphysic, has been proposed by W. H. V. Reade, Claude Tresmontant, and Edmond La B. Cherbonnier.[47] The latter quotes Tresmontant as follows:

> Certain metaphysical requirements are implied, organically proposed, by the [Biblical] revelation. They provide the metaphysical substructure appropriate to the theological message of the Holy Scriptures. This theological message may not be expressed in any metaphysic whatsoever; it cannot be embodied indiffferently in any structure of thought whatever. Platonism, for example, was radically unable to receive and transmit the Biblical theology of creation, incarnation, and real presence. . . . The various aspects of Hebraic thought do not comprise a rhapsody of contingent elements, fortuitously thrown together . . . rather they comprise the organically related parts of a coherent, systematic whole, a logically consistent structure of thought. . . . Consequently conversion to Christianity or Judaism requires a metaphysical conversion which abandons the pantheistic metaphysics of paganism in exchange for the Biblical metaphysic.[48]

45. Newman, *Tracts for the Times*, 1:iv.

46. See Zaehner, *Mysticism Sacred and Profane*, 204–5.

47. For a summary of this latter proposal, see Cherbonnier, "Is There a Biblical Metaphysic?"

48. Ibid., 458.

Wakefield notes that in the last century there has been "an immense interest in mysticism," which has resulted in the rediscovery of the English mystics of the fourteenth century: Richard Rolle, the author of *The Cloud of Unknowing*, Walter Hilton, Julian of Norwich, and Margery Kempe, most of whom stood in the tradition influenced by Platonism.[49] This development has been interpreted by W. R. Inge in his Bampton Lectures, *Christian Mysticism*, and by Evelyn Underhill in her book *Mysticism*.[50] This revival of interest in mysticism has been strengthened by the new Romantic movement, which arose in the 1960s.[51] This, however, has been balanced by a renewed commitment to the social gospel including the commitment to justice and peace. This was led by V. A. Demant who stated that there must be a gospel for society as well as for the individual, Maurice Reckitt, founder of the Christendom Group dedicated to the study of sociology, and William Temple who affirmed that it was the right and the responsibility of Christians to act in the light of Christian principles in the sphere of politics and enonomics.[52]

How has this division among Anglicans about the influence of the Platonist tradition, as well as other differences mentioned above, been treated? Although there has always been some squabbling among between different parties and traditions on this issue, it has been an element of the Anglican goal of comprehensiveness and of seeking a *via media* to make progress toward achieving two goals. First, wise Anglican leaders have always emphasized the importance and possibility of respecting alternate views of the interpretation of the Christian life, and, second, of the importance and possibility of adherents of different views engaging in open, honest, and serious conversation on such issues. In this way various forms of synthesis have been achieved. A perfect example of these goals and this process is spelled out in the Introduction to the report of the Doctrine Commission of the Church of England by the Chairman, William Temple, Archbishop of Canterbury. He states, concerning the spirit of the gatherings,

---

49. See the summary analysis of these figures in Thornton, *English Spirituality*, chs. 15–18.

50. See Ibid., 282–83.

51. See chapter 3.

52. See Wakefield, *Christian Spirituality*, 286–87.

We have become a company of personal friends. . . . It is truly said that to become bitter in controversy is more heretical than to espouse with sincerity and charity most devastating theological opinions. . . . We have been very frank in our comments to one another; brutally frank at times, were it not for the friendship which secured us against all risk of being 'wounded' or 'hurt.' . . . The authoritative value of agreement or *consensus* in doctrine depends upon the freedom of those who agree, so that the utmost liberty of thought compatible with maintenance of spiritual fellowship should be secured.[53]

53. See the "Chairman's Introduction," in *Doctrine in the Church of England*, 1–2.

CHAPTER TWO

Some Problems in Contemporary Christian Spirituality

IN THE HUGE BURGEONING of writing and activity in the area of Christian spirituality in the last two decades I believe that there are some very serious confusions and misunderstandings. They concern confusions in the definition and scope of spirituality, and misunderstandings deriving from English usage, the relation of spirituality and religion, inner and outer life, and private and public life. I will attempt to resolve these with some help from my teacher, Paul Tillich, among others.

I can summarize the main confusions and misunderstandings in the following way. It is commonly assumed that spirituality is an optional matter, that some people are more spiritual than others and some not at all, that spirituality is essentially a good thing (the more spirituality the better), that while spirituality is somehow related to religion it should be sharply distinguished from religion as something superior to and more important than religion, that spirituality is essentially a matter of the inner or interior life (while religion is a matter of the outer life), and that therefore spirituality is essentially concerned with private life rather than public life. In brief, I believe that these common assumptions are erroneous and lead to damaging results in contemporary spirituality. I should add, of course, that these confusions and misunderstandings are not universal. My point is that they are widespread.

As against these assumptions I believe that spirituality is something universally human, that all people are spiritual, that spirituality and religion are practically synonymous, that spirituality, therefore, is as much concerned with the outer life (of the body, community, institutions, liturgy, tradition, doctrine, ethics, and society) as with the inner, and that spirituality is as much concerned with the public life of citizenship and work as with private life.

First, the matter of definition and scope. I suspect that a large part of the problem here lies in the fact that the term "spirituality" is relatively new. Although it was apparently coined in the seventeenth century (when it was used pejoratively!) and has been used occasionally since then, it has come into common usage only in the last two or three decades. (The 1971 edition of the *Oxford English Dictionary* does not list the contemporary meaning.) Because of this relative novelty, it seems to have been assumed that "spirituality" must be distinct from religion or the Christian life, or that it is some special aspect of the Christian life.

I believe, however, that spirituality is most fruitfully defined as of all the uniquely human capacities and functions: self, self-transcendence, memory, anticipation, rationality (in the broadest sense), creativity, plus the moral, intellectual, social, political, aesthetic, and religious capacities, all understood as embodied. As Paul Tillich has put it, "Man's whole life, including his sensual life, is spiritual."[1]

(This is based on Tillich's definition of "spirit" as the unity of depth and form or power and meaning, and the *telos* of life. This in turn is elaborated as the unity of the two sides of the three polarities of ontological elements, power [individualization, dynamics, and freedom] and meaning [participation, form, and destiny]).[2]

This is the formal definition of spirituality. The material definition is the manifold forms in which these capacities and functions have been actualized in human history, namely, the variety of convictions, commitments, associations, and practices by which people have realized, interpreted, ordered, and guided their lives.

The upshot of this definition is that spirituality is universal and not optional. All people are spiritual. Hitler is just as spiritual as Mother Teresa. Spirituality can be good or bad, life-entrancing or life-destructive. Thus spirituality should not be used as an honorific but as a descriptive term. If this sounds odd to the reader, it is probably the result of the un-

---

1. Tillich, *Systematic Theology*, 2:51.
2. Ibid., 1:249f.

usually narrow meaning of the English term "spirit," which I will address below.

This implies that spirituality is a broader and more inclusive term than religion, rather than the other way around. Many philosophers of religion, however, have adopted an analogously broader definition of religion, namely, that of Tillich. He defines religion as "ultimate concern," which he describes as "an abstract translation of the great commandment: 'You shall love the Lord your God with all your heart, and with all your soul and with all your mind, and with all your strength.'"[3]

An ultimate concern is unconditional, total, infinite, and transcends preliminary concerns. "Our ultimate concern is that which determines our being or not-being." Furthermore, "every human being exists in the power of an ultimate concern, whether or not he is fully conscious of it, whether or not he admits it to himself or others."[4]

This means that all people have a religion, that which functions in their lives in the same way as the traditional religions, namely, interpreting their experience and ordering and guiding their lives. It has been objected that Tillich's definition of religion makes everyone into a religious person. Tillich, however, is perfectly aware that many people are not religious in the traditional sense of being adherents of one of the world religions.

So we could continue to define religion in the traditional way. But that would obscure the fact to which Tillich's definition bears witness, namely, that religion or being religious is an essential dimension of human existence. John Dewey makes a similar point when he asserts that there is a religious attitude, outlook, and function, and that "whatever introduces genuine perspective is religious."[5] Moreover, one of the volumes in the *World Spirituality* series deals with secular spiritualities.[6]

To continue with Tillich's thesis, preliminary concerns can become the "bearers and vehicles" of an ultimate concern. "In and through every preliminary concern the ultimate concern can actualize itself."[7] Tillich states that every preliminary concern, every area of culture (linguistic,

3. Ibid., 1:11.
4. Ibid., 1:14, 24.
5. Dewey, *Common Faith*, 17, 24.
6. Van Ness, *Spirituality and the Secular Quest*.
7. Tillich, *Systematic Theology*, 1:13.

technical, cognitive, aesthetic, personal, communal) is informed and given meaning by the ultimate concern that is manifest in it. "Religion as ultimate concern, is the meaning-giving substance of culture, and culture is the totality of forms in which the basic concern of religion expresses itself. In abbreviation: religion is the substance of culture, and culture is the form of religion."[8] If this interpretation of religion is adopted it becomes clear that spirituality and religion are practically synonymous.

One of the main sources of confusion in writing in English about spirituality is linguistic. In all the Germanic and Romance languages the word "spirit" has the broad meaning suggested above. In English alone, which is derived from the Germanic and Romance languages via Anglo-Saxon, Latin, and French, the word "spirit" has a much narrower meaning and is limited to religion in the traditional sense and even to the non-cognitive aspects of religion, namely, those having to do with emotion and will. Tillich states, "The word 'spirit' . . . has almost disappeared from the English language as a significant philosophical term, in contrast to German, French and Italian, in which the words, *Geist, esprit*, and *spirito* have preserved their philosophical standing."[9] Tillich attributes this to the impact of the British empirical tradition that separated the cognitive functions of mind from the functions of emotion and will and identified "spirit" with the latter.[10] The result has been that "spirit" has come to refer to religion in the sense of one of the departments of life and culture and even to the non-rational aspects of religion, rather than to all of the uniquely human capacities and functions as ordered by an ultimate concern.

The uniqueness of English usage can be most easily illustrated by its contrast with German usage, since the impact of German philosophy and theology has been dominant in the English speaking world for the past two centuries. Hegel's *Phaenomenologie des Geistes* was translated in all the other Germanic and the Romance languages as "phenomenology of spirit," but in English it had to be translated as "phenomenology of mind." "Spirit" would have been too narrow. Also the German term *Geisteswissenschaften* is usually translated as "human sciences" (but can include the arts and humanities) and refers to psychology, sociology, an-

---

8. Tillich, *Theology of Culture*, 42.
9. Tillich, *Systematic Theology*, 1:249.
10. Ibid., 1:249f., 3:21–25.

thropology, and so forth. But it means literally "sciences of spirit." If you heard that phrase, you might think it referred to the study of religion in the traditional sense or even the study of spiritualism.[11]

These examples illustrate the narrowness of the English term and the linguistic burden and potential confusions under which we English speakers labor. The result is that when we speak of spirituality, we are understood to be speaking of religion as a department of life or even a special dimension of that. To be spiritual means to be religious in the traditional sense, rather than to be fully human in the sense of actualizing all the uniquely human capacities and functions ordered by an ultimate concern.

Popular usage today, however, makes a sharp distinction between spirituality and religion, a distinction in which religion is denigrated and spirituality honored. Recent surveys of religious attitudes have often come across the statement, "I'm probably not very religious, but consider myself a deeply spiritual person."[12] In response to an essay in which I suggested that spirituality and religion are practically synonymous, a former student and the founder and director of one of the oldest and largest centers for spiritual formation has written that we should "see religion as the container [or] platform for the spiritual life, which in its essence may be qualitatively different from the container, as the heart is from the skeleton."

Along with this honorific-pejorative distinction goes the assumption that whereas religion deals with the outer life, that is, institutions, traditions, practices, doctrines, and moral codes, spirituality treats of the inner life. These tendencies add more confusion to our understanding of spirituality today.

The last point should he pursued further. In the Christian tradition of writing about spirituality and also today there is a pervasive focus and emphasis on the inner or interior life as distinguished from the outer, bodily, communal, and cultural life. One thinks, for example, of *The Interior Castle* of Teresa of Avila and of Thomas á Kempis's *The Imitation of Christ* in which book two is entitled "Suggestions Drawing Us Toward the Inner Life."

---

11. Other examples are *Geistesgeschichte*, which means intellectual or cultural history, and *Geistesbildung*, which means culture.

12. See, for example, McGuire, "Mapping Contemporary American Spirituality," 1c.

More recently Thomas Merton in a circular letter to his friends in 1968 shortly before his death wrote, "Our real journey is interior; it is a matter of growth, deepening, and an ever greater surrender to the creative action of love and grace in our hearts."[13] Finally, in a recent study Michael Downey comments on contemporary currents in Christian spirituality as follows: "The common perception is still that spirituality is primarily concerned with the life of the soul, the inner life, one's prayer life, one's spiritual life, as a separate compartment of the Christian life. The tendency to equate the spiritual life with the interior life is particularly prevalent in our own day."[14]

I believe that this emphasis on the inner life in contemporary spirituality is fundamentally mistaken—philosophically, theologically, and ethically—and that it needs to be redressed not only to a more balanced view of the inner-outer relation, but also to an awareness that the outer life is the major source of the inner.[15]

The philosophical critique has been carried out by Ludwig Wittgenstein and Charles Taylor, the theological critique by Fergus Kerr, among others, and the ethical critique by Alasdair MacIntyre and implicitly by some liberation theologians. One of the main achievements of Wittgenstein in his later writings was to reverse the Cartesian view of human beings and to argue that the outer life—namely, the body, actions, customs, practices, community, and tradition, what he called the "facts of living" or the "forms of life"—is primary and the foundation of everything we call "inner." Taylor claims that the emphasis on the inner life is not universal but is largely a Western idea that comes from Augustine who got it from Plotinus. He believes that it is a historically limited mode of self-interpretation that has become dominant in the modern West to the point of aberration.[16]

Kerr argues that this emphasis on interiority is derived from the Orphic and Gnostic myth of the soul, which has fallen into exile in the body and the natural world and seeks to free itself and transcend the body and the natural world to achieve purity and true knowledge. He sees modern Christian theology and spirituality as deeply infected by

13. Quoted in Shannon, *Silent Lamp*, 2.

14. Downey, *Understanding Christian Spirituality*, 105.

15. For this and the following paragraphs, see Thomas, "Interiority and Christian Spirituality."

16. Taylor, *Sources of the Self*, 111, 131.

this dualistic religious and philosophical tradition.[17] Finally, MacIntyre sharply criticizes what he calls the "interiorization of the moral life" in medieval and modern Christian ethics. Physical, social, and political circumstances are considered to be essentially irrelevant to morality.[18]

The inner-outer distinction is a spatial metaphor, which is misleading and largely unintelligible. It is misleading because it implies that the inner life is more important than the outer life of the body, the community, and the larger society, which are the main sources of the inner life. It is probably unintelligible, since all the criteria and most of the sources of the inner life are found only in the outer life. A better metaphor can be found in the mathematics of multiple spaces and has been developed by Karl Heim. Then what we call the inner life can be referred to as another space or dimension of human life distinct from those of the space-time world.[19]

Tillich takes a different approach. He does not use the inner-outer distinction but rather affirms what he calls the "self-world structure" or the "subject-object structure of being," which he describes as the "basic ontological structure" and the "basic articulation of being." It is basic, because it is presupposed in the fundamental ontological question, What is being itself?[20]

Tillich states that the term "self" is more embracing than the term "ego," because "it includes the subconscious and the nonconscious 'basis' of the self-conscious 'ego' as well as self-consciousness."[21] Then he asserts that the self has an environment from which it is distinguished and to which it belongs. But the self transcends every environment and therefore has a world, which Tillich defines as "the structural whole which includes and transcends all environments."[22]

The elements that constitute the self-world structure, which Tillich describes as the second level of ontological concepts, share the polar character of this basic ontological structure. As mentioned above, they are individualization and participation, dynamics and form, and freedom

17. Kerr, *Theology After Wittgenstein*, 172ff.

18. MacIntyre, *After Virtue*, 168–72.

19. Heim, *Christian Faith and Natural Science*.

20. Tillich, *Systematic Theology*, 1:164.

21. Ibid., 1:169.

22. Ibid., 1:70.

and destiny. In these polarities the first elements express the self-relatedness of being and the second the character of being part of a world. Furthermore, self and world are completely interdependent; there is no self without a world and no world without a self.[23] I believe that Tillich's concept of the self-world structure is a more fruitful approach to this issue than the inner-outer distinction.

The emphasis on the inner life in contemporary Christian spirituality is associated with a further distinction. Religion and spirituality are usually understood today to deal primarily with individual life, or at most with family life, with private life as distinguished from public life. This is indicated by the fact that today almost all of the resources of the churches (as well as institutes of spirituality), that is, personnel, funds, organizations, and so forth, are devoted to the private lives of individuals and the work of residential congregations that focus their attention and ministry primarily on the private family life of their members as distinct from their public life as citizens and workers.[24]

I believe that it is clear from Scripture, however, that the mission of the Church is to cooperate in God's mission to the world, the world that God creates, loves, judges, and wills to reconcile to God and lead to its fulfillment in God. Thus the mission of the Church is to the whole world and especially to that part of the world that is outside the Church. I believe, therefore, that the residential parish is in the worst possible position to carry out this mission, because it is almost entirely limited to and focused on the private lives of its members as distinct from their public lives as workers and citizens.

This focus on private life is derived largely from the separation of private and public life during the industrial revolution and the decision of the Church, apparently without much reflection, to opt for private life. This was undoubtedly abetted by the emphasis of traditional spirituality on the inner life. The problem here is that private residential life today is at the passive receptive end of society. It is not a particular form of private life that determines the nature of our economic, political, and cultural life, but rather just the opposite. The result is that the tendency of Church education, pastoral care, and spiritual formation and direction to focus

---

23. Ibid., 1:165, 168–71.

24. For this and the following paragraphs, see chapter 4.

on issues of private family life is undercutting the mission of the Church to public life.

In a recent book James Hillman, the distinguished Jungian analyst and interpreter of Jung, claims that the prevalence of psychotherapy in the last half century has been a major source of the lack of political awareness and participation. It tends to take the strong emotions of rage and fear, which often derive from the public life of a person, and to treat them only as problems of the inner life, as problems of personal growth, thus cutting them off from their relation to public life.[25] I believe that the same can be said of much pastoral care and spiritual direction today. A further difficulty is that private residential life is the area of modern life that is most thoroughly segregated by race, ethnic background, social class, and economic status. Thus residential parishes tend to emphasize homogeneity and resist diversity. This makes the addressing of problems of social and economic injustice extremely difficult.

Then there is the problem of clericalism, which is exacerbated in the residential parish, because there the functions of the clergy—namely, worship, preaching, sacraments, instruction, and pastoral care—are at the center of attention. Furthermore, the clergy often ask lay people to assist them in their (clerical) ministry. The implicit message is that if you want to take the Christian life seriously and actively, then you should model your life on that of the clergy. This reinforces the emphasis on private and family life to the exclusion of public life. This in turn undercuts the mission of the Church to public life, since it is primarily lay people who are in a position to carry this out.

Finally, private residential life is highly structured by gender. In a patriarchal society it is seen as the feminine realm as distinguished from public life that is understood to be the masculine realm. Therefore, any attempt coming from the private sector to influence the public sector will be resisted for strong cultural reasons. For all these reasons, and especially the emphasis on the inner life and the private life, the modern residential parish, to which the churches are devoting most of their resources, is seriously weakened in its mission to the whole of life.

I have suggested that these confusions and misunderstandings have damaging results in contemporary Christian spirituality, and I have implied what these are. If spirituality is optional, you can ignore it. If it is a

25. See Hillman and Ventura, *We've Had a Hundred Years*, 5 et passim.

matter of degree, then pride will enter in the form of claiming to be more spiritual than these "religious" people. If it is distinct from and superior to religion, then churches and their traditions, doctrines, ethics, institutions, and practices can be safely ignored. If spirituality is a matter of the inner life, then you do not need to bother yourself with all those boring and tiresome things of the outer life, such as the body, the community, and society. If spirituality is focused on the individual private life, then you can ignore all those troublesome and non-spiritual issues of public life in politics and economics.[26]

In sum, it is clear that these results are closely associated. They constitute a movement of Christian spirituality away from the public world toward the private world and also away from the outer world of the community and society and their institutions toward the interior life of the soul. Needless to say, the individual private life and the inner life are important subjects of Christian attention, interpretation, and ministry. It is the exclusive emphasis on them and their isolation from outer life and public life, which is the distortion. For this involves a serious misunderstanding of the Bible and the Christian tradition whose central themes are creation, incarnation, church, history, and the fulfillment of the creation in a transformation including the resurrection of the body.

William Temple, the most distinguished Archbishop of Canterbury of the past millennium, for quibblers at least since Anselm, made this point in his statement that Christianity is "the most avowedly materialist of all the great religions. . . . Its own most central saying is: 'The Word was made flesh,' where the last term was, no doubt, chosen because of its specifically materialist associations. By the very nature of its central doctrine Christianity is committed to a belief in the ultimate significance of the historical process, and in the reality of matter and its place in the divine scheme."[27]

I believe that the tendencies in contemporary Christian spirituality that I have described are a recrudescence in modern form of the gnosticism of the early Christian centuries. For example, Irenaeus, who was

26. In this connection a former student and experienced parish minister responded to an earlier draft by suggesting that in his experience much that passes for spirituality today is in fact a middle- and upper-middle-class luxury, indulgence, cop-out, and escape from the problems of the world.

27. Temple, *Nature, Man and God*, 478. See also *Christus Veritas* and *Christianity and Social Order*.

Bishop of Lyons in the second century and wrote a major treatise against gnosticism, saw references to the "inner man" as an essential theme of gnosticism. He stated that "the inner man may ascend on high in an invisible manner, as if their body was left among created things in this world."[28]

Today this gnosticism informs many of the New Age and other religious movements that appeared in the sixties as well as some movements from the last century, such as theosophy. This is often referred to as the perennial philosophy, which I believe to be the main alternative to mainline Judaism and Christianity in the United States today, rather than secular humanism, as is often supposed.[29] Furthermore, in an odd but very suggestive book Harold Bloom, the literary critic, goes much further and has argued that the real American religion is and always has been in fact this gnosticism, and the aspects of it to which he points are exactly the ones I have noted in contemporary Christian spirituality. He states, "The American Religion, for its two centuries of existence, seems to me irretrievably Gnostic. It is a knowing, by and of an uncreated self, or self-within-the-self, and the knowledge leads to freedom, a dangerous and doom-eager freedom: from nature, time, history, community, other selves. . . . [We are] an obsessed society wholly in the grip of a dominant Gnosticism."[30]

Moreover, it is important to note that the cultural context in which the recent burgeoning of interest in spirituality has taken place is the current romantic movement, which first emerged in the sixties in the youth counterculture movement. Theodore Roszak, author of *The Making of a Counter Culture*, has argued extensively that the essential foundation of this romantic movement is what he calls "the Old Gnosis." His interpretation of this phrase is rather vague, but one of his key examples is the idealistic monism of William Blake who drew on the "Neoplatonic-Hermetic myth" in the gnostic tradition."[31]

---

28. Irenaeus *Against the Heresies* I, 21, 4–5; Roberts, *Ante-Nicene Fathers*, 2:346b.

29. See the chapter titled "Christianity and the Perennial Philosophy," and the references therein to works by Robert S. Ellwood Jr. and Theodore Roszak, in Thomas, *What is it that Theologians Do.*

30. Bloom, *American Religion*, 49; see chapters 1, 2, 16. See also idem, *Omens of the Millennium*, Introduction, Prelude, and chapter 5.

31. Roszak, *Where the Wastland Ends*, 309, et passim. See also Ahlstrom, "Romaticism as a Religious Revolution," 3n, where he lists the "pronounced romantic interests that

What can we do to overcome these damaging results for Christian spirituality? First of all, we have a major task of reformulating much of the content of Christian formation, namely, baptismal and confirmation instruction and adult education on the Christian faith and life, as well as preaching, liturgy, and education for mission, along the lines I have suggested above.[32] Within this reformulation there must be, first, a renewed emphasis in Christian formation on the significance of the body and the material, social, economic, political, and historical world rather than an exclusive focus on the soul or interior life. This emphasis is obviously founded on the centrality in Christian faith of the themes of creation, incarnation, history, and consummation, including the resurrection of the body. Although there has been considerable attention devoted to the body in recent Christian spirituality; it has been largely focused on using the body as a foil for the progress of the soul.

Second, the reign of God must become central again in Christian spirituality. The reign of God is the fundamental theme of Jesus's mission: its inbreaking and manifestation in Jesus's presence, healing, and teaching. To be a follower of Jesus means to repent and open oneself to the presence of this reign, to look for and point to signs of the reign, and to participate in it by manifesting its signs in active love of the neighbor and in the struggle for justice and peace. The presence of the reign of God is manifest primarily in outer life and public life, as well as in inner life and private life, and it is the former that has been largely ignored in recent Christian formation. This has been abetted, for example, by the tendency to interpret *entos* in Luke 17:21 ("The Kingdom of God is among you.") as "within," whereas the overwhelming majority of exegetes agree that it means "among."[33]

Tillich made the reign of God fundamental in his theology, devoting the final main part of his *Systematic Theology* to it. This is the part

mark the sixties." He also describes "the principles of subjective interiority, the inward concern" as one of the main themes of romanticism (4) See also Fleischner, *Auschwitz: Beginning of a New Era?*, in which one section is entitled "The New Romanticism and Biblical Faith." In a chapter in the section Edith Wyschogrod refers to Neoplatonism and Vedanta as sources of the new romanticism.

32. For a further elaboration of the following points, see Thomas, "Interiority and Christian Spirituality."

33. See the extended discussion of this question by Fitzmeyer, *The Gospel According to Luke*, 1160–62.

entitled "History and the Kingdom of God" in which the reign of God is interpreted as the answer to the question about the meaning of history.[34]

Such emphasis on the reign of God will require attention to something that is rarely, if ever, included in Christian formation, namely, instruction in our responsibility to and means of access to the political process. By this I mean the whole political process from running for public office, seeking good candidates, campaigning, keeping in touch with elected officials, and if necessary using legal means to redress injustice. (I regularly inquire of directees if they know who their municipal, state, and national representatives and senators are and how they have voted recently on important issues.) If the primary axiom of Christian ethics is love of neighbor, and if our neighbor is anyone whose life we can affect by our actions, including our political actions, then for U. S. citizens our neighbors today include everyone in the world.

Third, there must be a primary emphasis on practice in Christian formation. The priority of practice in the Christian life has a long history. The Johannine Christ teaches that those who do the truth will know the truth. The Matthean Christ teaches that we will be judged on the basis of how we have responded to the need of our neighbors. It has usually been a principle of catholic theology that it is the practice of the Christian life that leads to the understanding of the Christian faith rather than the other way around. George Lindbeck has argued that a religion is like a set of acquired skills, a communal phenomenon that shapes subjectivities. So it is the practices of a religion that shape the inner life rather than the other way around.[35]

The priority of practice suggests that Christian formation should focus on public worship, the building up of the community, the service of those in need, and participation in the struggle for justice and peace. This does not mean that the traditional practices of silence, mental prayer, meditation, and contemplation should be ignored, but only that they should be balanced by attention to communal and public practice. In any case, if prayer and meditation are authentic, they are practiced in the larger context of public worship and community life, and they lead directly to participation in public life.

34. See Tillich, *Systematic Theology*, 3: pt 5. For another elaboration of the importance of the reign of God, see Sobrino, *Spirituality of Liberation*, chapter 7.

35. Lindbeck, *The Nature of Doctrine*, 33ff.

It may have occurred to many Anglicans that their spirituality should be somewhat more immune to the confusions and misunderstandings mentioned above than some other Christian traditions, as is suggested by the quotation from Temple. This possible immunity derives from the traditional Anglican emphasis on the doctrines of creation, incarnation, church, and sacramental life, as well as the sense of responsibility for public life deriving originally from the (otherwise dubious) establishment of the Church of England.

It may seem odd, therefore, to use a German Lutheran as a primary source for the above critique of contemporary spirituality. This should not be surprising, however, in light of the fact that Lutheranism was a major influence on the development of Anglicanism in the sixteenth century. Moreover, many Anglican theologians have been struck by what has seemed to them to be the Anglican flavor of Tillich's theology.

This can be seen at many points; for example, in Tillich's commitment to the Bible as the "basic source" and "formal norm" of theology, in his massive knowledge and use of the theological tradition of the Church, in his emphasis on reason and the rational character of theology, in his stress on experience as the transformative medium through which the sources of theology are received and on the "experiential verification" of faith and theology, in his critical use of philosophy, and finally in his emphasis on political and economic life in the Christian interpretation of history.[36] Anglicans have especially noted Tillich's emphasis on the balance of what he called the "catholic substance" and the "protestant principle."[37]

It may not be widely known, moreover, that Tillich had a major impact on the Episcopal Church in the past half century in two ways. First, many of the last generation of theologians in the Episcopal Church were deeply influenced by Tillich: A. T. Mollegen, Clifford Stanley, Norman Pittenger, William Wolf, and myself, among others. Second, in the first *Church's Teaching Series* published in the forties the volume on theology was written by Pittenger and James Pike who was also influenced by Tillich. This volume, which informed the Church's teaching for a generation, contained many themes.[38]

36. See Tillich, *Systematic Theology*, 1:35, 46, 53–59, 102, pt I–I; 3 pt V–II, C.

37. Pittenger notes this theme in his essay, "Paul Tillich as a Theologian."

38. In this connection it may be noted that in one of the first symposia on Tillich's theology one third of the authors were Anglicans. See Kegley, *Theology of Paul Tillich*.

If the argument of this essay is valid, then we face a major task of reassessment of much of the theory and practice of Christian spirituality. This will involve a reformulation of the definition and scope of spirituality and its relation to religion, and a reformulation of the relation of inner and outer life and of private and public life in Christian spirituality. Some of this work has already begun, but it has coexisted with widespread confusions and misunderstandings of Christian spirituality. Only a renewed attention to these issues can bring to the theory and practice of Christian spirituality a new coherence.

CHAPTER THREE

Spiritual But Not Religious:
The Influence of the Current Romantic Movement

MANY COMMENTATORS HAVE NOTED the current cultural phenomenon of the large number of people, perhaps 20 percent of Americans, who are self-identified as "spiritual but not religious." Some of these commentators have offered explanations for this phenomenon. Among these are Weber's idea of the "routinization of charisma" in organized religion, which may have turned off many seekers; the regular emergence in the religious traditions of renewal movements of which the spirituality movement may be an example; the unprecedented contact and interchange among the world religions; the suspicion of institutions of all kinds and the resulting search for something more individual, private, and experiential; and the authoritarian structures and social constraints of religious institutions that have become hurtful and destructive.[1]

Since this phenomenon seems to be limited to English and North American cultures, another possible explanation of it is linguistic. I refer here to the fact that the meaning of "spirit" (and thus "spirituality") in English is much narrower than its equivalents in the Germanic and Romance languages, in which it refers to all the uniquely human

---

1. Maguire, "Mapping Contemporary American Spirituality"; Burton-Christie, "Retrieval"; Schneiders, "Religion vs. Spirituality"; Fuller, *Spiritual, but Not Religious*, 5–7; Roof, *Spiritual Marketplace*, 81–82, 173–79; and Locklin, *Spiritual but Not Religious?*, 2–5.

capacities and cultural functions.[2] Tillich attributes this difference to the impact of the British empirical tradition, which separated the cognitive functions of the mind from the functions of emotion and will, and identified "spirit" with the latter.[3] Thus *Geist* became "ghost" and *esprit* became "sprite." This may have led some to see a clear difference between religion and spirituality. This linguistic factor, however, has undoubtedly been enhanced by the explanation for the phenomenon of "spiritual but not religious" offered below.

In this essay I will propose that a major reason for this phenomenon, which has not been noted, is that the current spirituality movement that arose in the 1970s is largely the product of a new Romantic movement that emerged in the 1960s. The current Romantic movement has influenced all aspects of our cultural life; the spirituality movement is in large part a product of this. Romantic movements always tend to disparage traditional religion and to affirm unorthodox, exotic, individualistic spiritualities. Romantic movements are also ambiguous, with tendencies that are destructive as well as productive. This ambiguity also attaches to the current spirituality movement.

What are the marks of a Romantic movement? Philosopher William Thomas Jones has described Romanticism as a complex syndrome of "biases" in the direction of what he calls the dynamic, the disordered, the continuous, the soft-focused, the inner, and the otherworldly.[4] Historian Craig Brinton portrays the Romantic temperament as "sensitive, emotional, preferring color to form, the exotic to the familiar, eager for novelty, for adventure, above all for the vicarious adventure of fantasy, reveling in disorder and uncertainty, insistent on the uniqueness of the individual to the point of making a virtue of eccentricity." He states that Romanticism involves the "exaltation of intuition, spirit, sensibility; imagination, faith, the immeasurable, the infinite, the wordless."[5] Sociologist Colin Campbell, quoting Gauderfroy-Demombynes, states,

> Romanticism is a way of feeling, a state of mind in which *sensibilité* and imagination predominates over reason; it tends towards the new, towards individualism, revolt, escape, melancholy, and

2. For a fuller elaboration of this point, see p. 19.

3. See Paul Tillich, *Systematic Theology*, 1:249–50, 3:21–25.

4. Jones, *Romantic Syndrome*, chaps. 5–7.

5. Brinton, "Romanticism," 7:206b, 209b.

fantasy. Other typical characteristics of this way of feeling would be: dissatisfaction with the contemporary world, a restless anxiety in the face of life, a preference for the strange and curious, a penchant for reverie and dreaming, a leaning to mysticism, and a celebration of the irrational.[6]

The existence of a new Romantic movement has been argued by historians, sociologists, theologians, philosophers, and interpreters of popular culture. The historian Theodore Roszak has argued extensively that we are in a new Romantic movement in his books *The Making of a Counter Culture* (1969) and *Where the Wasteland Ends* (1972). He explores the youth movement of the 1960s and interprets it as a new Romantic movement by comparing it with the first Romantic movement of the late eighteenth and early nineteenth centuries. To support his thesis, Roszak offers an analysis of the themes of the first Romantic movement in the work of Blake, Wordsworth, and Goethe. Then he shows how these themes have been adopted by the youth movement, seen especially in its protest against the dominance of science and technology and the resulting rationalization, secularization, bureaucratization, and dehumanization of life.[7] Although Roszak refers solely to the German and English versions of the first Romantic movement, a similar case could be made from the American version as exemplified in the work of Ralph Waldo Emerson and the Transcendentalists, who were deeply influenced by the European versions.[8]

Roszak often appeals to Jung, especially in the latter's studies of hermeticism and alchemy. Philip Rieff offers an interpretation of romantic themes in Jung's writings, namely, feeling versus intellect, spontaneity versus restriction, the unconscious as savior, introversion, the creative disorder of the interior life, and especially fantasy, which Rieff describes as "the Jungian successor to Christian faith."[9]

Also, in an unpublished essay of 1971 entitled "Romanticism as a Religious Movement," historian Sydney Ahlstrom states,

> Many observers have pointed to a pronounced romantic element in the new interests that mark the 1960's. A short unelaborated

6. Campbell, *Romantic Ethic*, 181.

7. Roszak, *Making of a Counter Culture*; Roszak, *Where the Wasteland Ends*.

8. See Fuller, *Spiritual, but Not Religious*, 23–30.

9. Rieff, *Triumph of the Therapeutic*, 118.

enumeration will suffice as a reminder: 1) the revival of Novalis' plea that youth must bring in the new day; 2) the surge of interest in Far Eastern religion that Herder and Friedrich Schlegel pioneered; 3) the commitment to history that Hegel personified and which Herbert Marcuse and the Marxist revival betoken; 4) the renewed interest in astrology, hermetic philosophy, and the occult which Saint-Martin and Oetinger championed; 5) the interest in subjectivity, the subconscious, and openness to others associated with Rousseau's *Confessions* and dozens of romantic autobiographical expositions; 6) the search for the meaning and realization of an organic sense of community and a general enlivening of organic metaphors as an antidote to materialism, individualism, and mechanism; 7) a widespread attack on conventional morality which also reverberated in [Rousseau's] *La Nouvelle Heloise* and [Schlegel's] *Lucinda*; 8) a return of interest in Hermann Hesse who himself recapitulated many of these themes, not least a deep regard for Hölderlin; and 9) a new reverence for Nature.

Four British sociologists confirm the judgment of the historians. Bernice Martin states, "At the heart of the radical movement which will be the focus of my attention is the so-called 'counter-culture' of the late 1960s. My argument is that it served as a dramatic embodiment of certain crucial Romantic values which in the subsequent decades became intimately woven into the fabric of our culture."[10] Christopher Booker affirms a similar thesis and focuses on fantasy, one of the marks of Romanticism emphasized by Brinton, Campbell, and Rieff. Booker analyzes the stages of what he calls the "cycle of fantasy," and concludes: "In these five stages or moods of fantasy we have, in fact, . . . uncovered [in] the pattern of innumerable films, novels, plays, and stories, the basic Romantic legend, in which the pursuit of some kind of defiance or violation of order winds to its inevitable destruction."[11] Frank Musgrove states, "Nineteenth-century Romanticism was strikingly like the contemporary counter culture in its explicit attack on technology, work, pollution, boundaries, authority, the unauthentic, rationality, and the family. . . . But perhaps the most striking and significant similarity between the Romantics and today's counter culture is this: the imagination of today's counter culture feeds on science fiction. The Romantics invented it."[12] Compare, for ex-

10. Martin, *Sociology of Contemporary Cultural Change*, 2.

11. Booker, *Neophiliacs*, 73.

12. Musgrove, *Ecstasy and Holiness*, 65.

ample, Mary Shelley's *Frankenstein: A Modern Prometheus* (1818) and the movies *2001: A Space Odyssey, Star Wars, Lord of the Rings,* and *Spider Man,* among others.

In a 1977 volume on the Holocaust, there is a section entitled "The New Romanticism and Biblical Faith." In this section theologian Michael Ryan finds evidence of the new Romanticism in Charles Reich's book *The Greening of America* (1970) in which Consciousness I represents the old Romanticism, Consciousness II the technocratic managerial revolution, and the emerging Consciousness III, which rejects Consciousness II and reaffirms Consciousness I, that is, the new Romanticism. He finds further evidence in historian William Irwin Thompson's book *At the Edge of History* (1971), in which Thompson criticizes industrial society and calls for a deeper understanding of human life and history, which can be found in the myths of Atlantis and of Native Americans; in the prophecies of the famous psychic Edgar Cayce; the poetry of the great English Romantic William Blake; and the science fiction of J. R. R. Tolkien, C. S. Lewis, and Arthur Clarke, author of *2001: A Space Odyssey.*[13]

In the same section of this volume, philosopher Edith Wyschogrod contrasts Romantic consciousness and biblical faith by describing Romanticism as a metaphysics of consciousness, and biblical faith as a metaphysics of event. She claims that the former expands the role given to individual consciousness with the goal of unlimited freedom and the tendency to identify the self with God, as in Hegel. This leads Romanticism to an apotheosis of the undetermined, of chaos, and finally to a valorization of death, which, she argues, was the contribution of Romanticism to Nazism.[14] Theodore Roszak is also aware of this darker side of Romanticism. He warns that the new Romantic movement may lead to a "rampant, antinomian mania which . . . threatens to plunge us into a dark and savage age." Here he refers to Peter Viereck's book *Metapolitics: The Roots of the Nazi Mind* (1961), which he describes as a "thorough attempt to spell out the connections between Nazism and Romanticism."[15]

Closely associated with these manifestations of the new Romantic movement is a new intensity of consumerism. In 1970 psychoanalyst

13. Ryan, "New Romanticism and Biblical Faith," 290–92.

14. Edith Wyschogrod, "Romantic Consciousness and Biblical Faith," in Fleischner, *Auschwitz,* 131–342.

15. Roszak, *The Making of a Counter Culture,* 73.

Erich Fromm stated, "Man is in the process of becoming a *homo consumens*, a total consumer. . . . This vision of the total consumer is indeed a new image of man that is conquering the world."[16] Noting that American consumer debt now exceeds $2 trillion, one commentator states, "U. S. shopping centers now outnumber high schools and attract 20 million shoppers a month. In as many as a dozen states, the biggest tourist attraction is not a historical site or a cultural attraction: It's a mall. . . . The Nation's largest temple to malldom [is] the 4.2 million-square-foot Mall of America in Minnesota."[17] British sociologist Colin Campbell sees this consumerism as a manifestation of the current Romantic movement, even as the first Romantic movement facilitated the emergence of the consumerism that fueled the Industrial Revolution in the late eighteenth and early nineteenth centuries. He states that although consumption would seem to be at the opposite pole of life from Romanticism,

> [t]here is one significant modern phenomenon which does indeed directly connect the two. This, of course, is advertising, for even the most cursory examination of the pages of glossy magazines and the contents of television commercials will serve to reveal how many advertisements are concerned with the topic of "romance", or with images and copy which deal with scenes which are "remote from everyday experience", "imaginative" or suggestive of "grandeur" or "passion". [The phrases in quotation marks are from the definition of "romantic" in The Oxford English Dictionary.] And it is not just romance in the narrow sense which features so prominently in conjunction with perfume, cigarettes, or lingerie advertisements—it is also that the pictures and stories used are typically "romantic" in the broader sense of being exotic, imaginative and idealized; whilst the very purpose of advertisements, of course, is to induce us to buy the products which are featured: in other words to consume.[18]

There is also a great deal of evidence of a new Romantic movement in American popular culture today.[19] Picking up on Craig Brinton's

16. Fromm, "Problems of Surplus," 72.

17. Vicki Haddock, "Lessons in Human Buy-ology," *San Francisco Chronicle*, 19 December 2004, sec. D1. See also these important studies of the new consumerism: Schor, *Do Americans Shop Too Much?*; Schor, *Commercialized Child and the New Consumer Culture*; and Schor and Holt, *Consumer Society Reader*.

18. Campbell, *Romantic Ethic*, 1–2.

19. When I searched "new Romantic movement" on the Internet, in .07 seconds I re-

characterization of the Romantic longing "above all for the vicarious adventure of fantasy" (also mentioned by Rieff, Booker, and Campbell), I refer to the record-breaking popularity of such movie series as *Star Wars, Harry Potter, Lord of the Rings, King Arthur*, and *Spider Man*. Commenting on these, a movie critic concludes, "Perhaps more than ever before, Hollywood is an empire of fantasy." Another reviewer describes the devotees of *Harry Potter* as "obsessed, incurable die-hard romantics." Finally, a third reviewer summarizes the significance of the *Lord of the Rings* trilogy by stating, "They revive the art of Romantic wonder."[20]

The influence of the current Romantic movement can also be seen in the contemporary neoconservative movement that informs the administration of George W. Bush. The mentor of the neoconservative theorists and their disciples is the political philosopher Leo Strauss who taught at the University of Chicago in the middle of the last century. Strauss's impact has been described as the largest academic movement in the last century and he has been called the godfather of the Republican Party's Contract with America of 1994. Strauss's political thought shows the influence of the Romantic political philosophers Edmund Burke and Jean-Jacques Rousseau, and he praised Romanticism as the strongest German protest against liberal modernity. He was also influenced by the Romantic reactionaries Oswald Spengler, Carl Schmitt, Ernst Jünger, and Martin Heidegger. His thought is marked by several Romantic themes and tendencies: the esoteric character of his teaching, which has been described as kabbalistic; opposition to modernity; rule by a secret wise elite who are considered godlike; the state seen as sacred; a hierarchical ordering of society; antipathy to liberal democracy; abhorrence of egalitarianism; the importance of religion and moral law as the basis of society; and an emphasis on rootedness in the soil, and on militarism and war.[21] In this connection it may be noted that the first Romantics hailed Napoleon as a world historical figure, one whom Hegel called a "world

---

ceived 217,000 items treating the new Romanticism in art, architecture, music, literature, criticism, and so forth.

20. See A. O. Scott, "A Hunger for Fantasy, an Empire to Feed It," *New York Times*, June 16, 2002, Arts and Leisure section, 1; Bruce McCall, "Not Scared of Harry Potter," *New Yorker*, December, 10 2001, 54; Alex Ross, "The Ring and the Rings," *New Yorker*, December 22 and 29, 2003, 162b.

21. See Drury, *Leo Strauss and the American Right*, 2, 3, 41; Drury, *Alexandre Kojève*, 155; Drury, *Political Ideas of Leo Strauss*. Professor Drury has stated that she agrees with my interpretation of Strauss.

soul" I am suggesting that Strauss's political thought was influenced by the first Romantic movement and that its widespread influence today can be attributed, at least in part, to the current Romantic movement.

It should be noted that postmodernism in literary and cultural theory, which emerged in the 1960s, can also be considered to be an aspect of the current Romantic movement. Postmodern authors often refer to figures in the first Romantic movement, such as Goethe, Blake, Rousseau, Burke, Emerson, and Wordsworth, as forerunners of postmodernism. This is not surprising, since both movements involve a strong critique of the Enlightenment and neoclassical traditions. A study of postmodernism states that Romanticism is one of the movements that "form the backbone of a counter-Enlightenment tradition and are important influences on some versions of postmodern theory."[22]

I also find the influence of the current Romantic movement in contemporary Christian theology. Especially, among its younger practitioners, I find a suspicion of clarity, precision, analysis, and rationality, and a favoring of the Romantic themes of the vague, the complex, the irrational, the anarchic, the chaotic, the wild, the Dionysian, the exotic, the esoteric, the heretical, the ancient and primitive, the apophatic, the holistic, the mystical, and the divine darkness. For example, in 1980 the dean of an Episcopal seminary published an essay on theology and religious renewal that exemplifies the current Romantic movement. He states that renewal requires us "to move, at times, to the edge of chaos," to have "a confrontation with the abyss." "Felt and intuitive meaning borders on chaos, whereas thinking is several steps removed from chaos." Theology and religion need "the willingness to get dirty together." Also he calls us to embrace "the threat" and "the antistructural." "We must intentionally move into the darkness, the surd, the unknown behind our systems." He offers three illustrations of the darkness into which we must intentionally move: "our grim fear of our own sexuality"; the need in the liturgy for the archaic, the bizarre, and the vulgar; and "formation in the wilderness."[23]

Both Jones and Brinton mention a bias toward the disordered or a reveling in disorder as marks of a Romantic movement. An example of

---

22. Best, *Postmodern Turn*, 29.

23. Holmes, "Theology and Religious Renewal," 3–19, at 16–19. See also McCord, "Editorial: The Blurred Vision," in which he refers to our "moving out of one age into another," and to one reaction to this as the "romantic left" which, in its fears of the "promised land of technology," represents a "flourishing romanticism."

this in recent theology is an increasing fascination with chaos theory in physics and a major revival of the idea of creation out of chaos in a number of books and articles. I will mention three of them. In his book *Chaos Theology: A Revised Creation Theology* (2002), Sjoerd Bonting considers the implications of chaos theory for various topics in theology. In James Huchingson's book *Pandemonium Tremendum: Chaos and Mystery in the Life of God*, all of the Romantic themes appear. He states. "The chaos [that is, the Pandemonium Tremendum] is the Ungrund, the fundament and basis of the divine life, the ground and Groundlessness of God, eternal and uncaused, at once the answer to the cosmological question and the most profound mystery."[24] In Catherine Keller's book *Face of the Deep: A Theology of Becoming*, again all the Romantic themes appear and many Romantic heroes are cited, such as Dionysius, Eckhart, Blake, Schelling, and the "Cloud" author. She states, "The tehomic deity [a reference to *tehom* or deep in Gen 1:2] remains enmeshed in the vulnerabilities and potentialities of an indeterminate creativity. As *Tehom* it is that process; as deity it is born from and suckles that process."[25] The theological problem with these views, apart from lack of clarity, is pointed out by Paul Ricoeur, who interprets this approach as one of the four great myths of the origin of evil in which evil is identified with the chaos out of which the world is made. Thus evil is built into the order of things. It is not a matter of human responsibility, and it is irredeemable.[26] I believe that this fascination with chaos shows the influence of the current Romantic movement.[27]

For our purposes, however, I believe that the main evidence of the current Romantic movement is found in the current spirituality movement that emerged in the 1970s and has become a vast multimillion dollar industry involving thousands of full-time professional specialists, many new spiritual formation centers, a large number of new professorial

24. Huchingson, *Pandemonium Tremendum*, 132.

25. Keller, *Face of the Deep*, 226. See also Hefner, "God and Chaos: The Demiurge versus the Ungrund"; and Chandler, "When the World Falls Apart: Method for Employing Chaos and Emptiness as Theological Constructs."

26. Ricoeur, *Symbolism of Evil*, part 2, chap. 1.

27. Some attempts have been made to employ chaos theory in explaining divine action in the world, but it is a minority view since the equations of chaos theory are deterministic. See Russell, *Chaos and Complexity* and Thomas, "Chaos, Complexity, and God: A Review Essay."

chairs of spirituality in seminaries and other graduate schools, a large new publishing enterprise producing hundreds of new books on spirituality every year, and the creation of new sections on spirituality in almost all bookstores.[28] Two British scholars of religion have stated, "Spirituality is big business. . . . We now see the introduction of modes of 'spirituality' into educational curricula, bereavement and addiction counseling, psychotherapy and nursing. Spirituality as a cultural trope has also been appropriated by corporate bodies and management consultants to promote efficiency, extend markets, and maintain a leading edge in a fast-moving information economy."[29] A researcher and analyst of business trends has stated, "Spirituality is today's greatest megatrend."[30]

Now there is, of course, some overlap between the spirituality movement and the continuing tradition of the churches' teaching about and formation in the Christian life. They shade into each other. In my judgment, an organization such as the Society for the Study of Christian Spirituality represents primarily the continuing tradition of the churches' practice, whereas an organization such as Spiritual Directors International represents the spirituality movement.

I believe that the marks of the current spirituality movement include many of those of the first Romantic movement mentioned by Jones, Brinton, and Campbell. I will focus on a few of them: an emphasis on the interior life as distinct from the outer life of the body, the community, and history; a focus on individual and private life rather than public life; an emphasis on feeling rather than rationality; and finally, our main topic, a sharp distinction between religion that is disparaged and spirituality that is honored. Along with these go a fascination with the ancient, the primitive, the exotic, the esoteric, the mystical, the mysterious, the apophatic, and the heretical. All of these, I believe, characterize the current spirituality movement and the new Romantic movement of which it is in large part a product.[31] In his book *Spiritual, but Not Religious* (2001), Robert C. Fuller notes that a contemporary survey indicates that those self-identified as "spiritual but not religious" were "associated with higher

---

28. See Schneiders, "Religion vs. Spirituality," 163.
29. Carrette, *Selling Spirituality*, 1.
30. Aburdene, *Megatrends 2070*, 6; see also ch. 1.
31. See chapter 2.

levels of interest in mysticism, experimentation with unorthodox beliefs and practices, and negative feelings toward both clergy and churches."[32]

Both the current spirituality and Romantic movements strongly emphasize the importance and centrality of interiority or the interior life. W. T. Jones has noted the centrality of interiority in the first Romantic movement.[33] One of the most important publications of the current spirituality movement is the twenty-five-volume series entitled *World Spirituality*. In the "Preface to the Series" in each of the volumes, the general editor, Ewart Cousins, states, "This series focuses on that inner dimension of the person called by certain traditions 'the spirit.' This spiritual core is the deepest center of the person."[34] In a 1992 study, Michael Downey comments, "The common perception is still that spirituality is primarily concerned with the life of the soul, the inner life, one's prayer life, one's spiritual life, as a separate compartment of the Christian life. The tendency to equate the spiritual life with the interior life is particularly prevalent in our own day."[35]

Second, both the current Romantic and spirituality movements focus on individual and private life rather than communal and public life. In noting this emphasis in the first Romantic movement, historian Jack Forstman states that the early German Romantics were "overwhelmed and exhilarated by the awareness of individuality."[36] This appears in the current Romantic and spirituality movements in a similar focus on individual private life rather than public life. Any suggestion that spirituality has anything to do with public issues is extremely rare.[37]

A similar case can be made for the emphasis in the current Romantic and spirituality movements on feeling, passion, and sentiment rather than rationality. In Goethe's *Faust*, which Jacques Barzun describes as "the Bible of the [first] Romantic movement," the hero cries "Feeling is

32. Fuller, *Spiritual, but Not Religious*, 6.

33. See Jones, *Romantic Syndrome*, 125–26.

34. Cousins, *World Spirituality*.

35. Downey, *Understanding Christian Spirituality*, 105. I have criticized the concept of interiority in my essay "Interiority and Christian Spirituality."

36. Forstman, *Romantic Mangle*, xii.

37. See Thomas, "Political Spirituality: Oxymoron or Redundancy?" Once, in a lecture on spirituality to a group of scholars, I mentioned that I usually inquired of directees if they knew the names of their municipal, state, and national representatives and how they had voted on recent important issues, which I consider to be an essential discipline of the Christian life. The response was incredulous laughter, thus confirming my point.

all". This has been strongly echoed in the current Romantic and spirituality movements in the focus on feeling, emotion, and sensitivity originally exemplified in the human potential movement and in the work of the National Training Laboratories and the Esalen Institute.

A new study brings together three themes of the current Romantic movement that have been discussed above: spirituality, consumerism, and neoconservatism. The authors argue that the spirituality movement has been taken over and further individualized, privatized, and commodified by what they call neoliberal (that is, economic neoconservative) multinational, corporate capitalism in order to sell its worldview and its products. This has removed any concern in spirituality for community, social justice, or politics. Such privatization and commodification has been accomplished through contemporary humanistic psychology and the colonization of Asian religious traditions in New Age forms. In order to further the goals of neoliberal corporate capitalism, this individualized and privatized spirituality is now widely used in educational and professional institutions, including health care, counseling, business training, management theory, and marketing.[38]

Both the Romantic and the Spirituality movements manifest a fascination with the ancient, the exotic, the esoteric, the mystical, and the heretical. This is represented in the first Romantic movement by Novalis's devotion to Plotinus and Boehme and his idealization of the Middle Ages, by Schopenhauer's adherence to Vedanta, and Goethe's commitment to Neoplatonism and Gnosticism. In the current Romantic movement, there is the newfound interest of Protestants in such figures and movements as the Desert Fathers, Celtic spirituality, and the medieval mystics. Then there is the widespread popularity of the new multivolume series *Classics of Western Spirituality*, which includes *The Cloud of Unknowing*, Pseudo-Dionysius, Jakob Boehme, and Emmanuel Swedenborg.

This fascination is perfectly exemplified in the current widespread interest in the Kabbalah, the collection of texts of medieval Jewish mysticism with alleged sources in the second century. The Kabbalah arose in Provence in the thirteenth century and was influenced by Neoplatonist and Gnostic traditions. A recent newspaper article described the Kabbalah as "arcane, obscure, and inaccessible. . . . Its inaccessibility is what

38. See Carrette, *Selling Spirituality*.

makes it attractive."[39] The Kabbalah has been taken up in varying degrees by celebrities such as Madonna, Barbra Streisand, Courtney Love, Roseanne Barr, Britney Spears, Demi Moore, Paris Hilton, Winona Ryder, Elizabeth Taylor, and Mick Jagger. It is promoted by the Kabbalah Centre International, which has twenty-three offices worldwide and claims eighteen thousand students in its classes, ninety thousand members in the United States, and ninety thousand visits to its website every month. The Kabbalah as ancient, exotic, esoteric, mystical, and heretical is a perfect example and vehicle of the current Romantic and spirituality movements. The 2001 Annual Meeting of Spiritual Directors International had workshops on the Kabbalah, as well as on the sacred labyrinth and the Enneagram, and on "Praying through the great elements of Earth/Air/Fire Water."[40]

Now I turn to our main topic: the contemporary cultural phenomenon of those who identify themselves as spiritual but not religious, and the related tendency to disparage religion and to honor spirituality. This was typical of the first Romantic movement, and is exemplified in the subtitle of Schleiermacher's great Romantic work *On Religion: Speeches to Its Cultured Despisers*. The term "Despisers" was a reference primarily to Schleiermacher's friends Schlegel and Novalis, the leaders of the first German Romantic movement, who did in fact despise traditional organized religion and had turned toward Gnosticism and theosophy.[41] Similarly, Goethe, the father of German Romanticism, early rejected what he called positive, that is traditional, religion. He was fascinated with the heretics and developed a personal religion based on Neoplatonism and modeled on Valentinian Gnosticism.[42] Cyril O'Regan considers the main example of Gnostic return in England to be the Romantic poet William Blake, who was deeply influenced by Jakob Boehme and Emmanuel Swedenborg and departed from traditional Christianity.[43] This attitude is echoed in the current Romantic and spirituality movements.

Roszak holds that traditional Christianity is not the solution but rather part of the problem, and he finds the basis of both the old and

39. Yollin, "New Interest in Jewish Mysticism."

40. For a more extended argument for the existence of a new Romantic movement, see chapter 5, *What is it that Theologians Do*.

41. See Forstman, *Romantic Triangle*, chs. 2 and 3.

42. See Goethe, *Autobiography of Johann Wolfgang von Goethe*, 379–82.

43. See O'Regan, *Gnostic Return in Modernity*; and O'Regan, *Gnostic Apocalypse*.

the new Romanticism in what he calls "the old Gnosis," which includes the hermetic, magical, alchemical, astrological, and occult traditions; Islamic and Hindu mysticism; Kabbalah; Zen; I Ching; Tarot; Taoism; chakra yoga; Buddhist tantra; and ancient Gnosticism. This is taken to an extreme in Diarmuid Ó Murchú, a former Roman Catholic monk and a leader of the spirituality movement, who was the keynote speaker at the annual conference in 2002 of Spiritual Directors International, the largest professional group at the heart of the spirituality movement, with over four thousand members. According to Ó Murchú, spirituality emerged forty thousand years ago in the Paleolithic period as "a cosmological synthesis imbued with a highly developed holistic, intuitive and spiritual consciousness" devoted to the worship of the Great Mother Goddess. Religion, however, appeared only five thousand years ago and has been the source of all of our alienation and inhumanity. "Religion in its essential essence is about alienation from the Earth and the cosmos." "Religion thrives on perpetuating that state of exile and alienation." The end of religion is "a likely possibility and a highly desirable one." Ó Murchú hails "the probable decline of formal religion and the revival of spirituality."[44]

In general in the current Romantic movement, and to some extent in the spirituality movement, traditional Christianity is often seen as a grand conspiracy against anything new, fascinating, and heterodox. This is exemplified, for example, in the wide popularity of Elaine Pagels's books *The Gnostic Gospels* (1979) and *Beyond Belief: The Secret Gospel of Thomas* (2003); and especially in the 2003 runaway fiction best-seller *The Da Vinci Code* by Dan Brown, whose theme is the marriage of Jesus to Mary Magdalene, the birth of their child, and the desperate suppression of all this by some churches. A spokesperson for Doubleday has stated that it is "the fastest-selling adult book of all time." It has sold over sixty million copies and has been on the bestseller list for over two years. Furthermore, it has been succeeded by two copycat best-sellers: *The Rule of Four* and *The Historian*.

It should be noted that there is an important difference between the two Romantic movements in their attitude toward science. In its emphasis on disorder and uncertainty, the first Romantic movement attacked the Newtonian science celebrated by the Enlightenment. This was more the case in England than in Germany, where Goethe and Schopenhauer

44. Ó Murchú, *Religion in Exile*, viii, 14, 29, 65, 66.

had some interest in and knowledge of science. In England, however, Blake and Wordsworth in particular were unremitting in their attack on Newtonian empirical science. In the current Romantic movement, however, the attitude toward science has been occasionally more affirmative. The main reason for this has been the emergence early in the last century of what has been called postmodern science, in particular relativity and quantum theory and later chaos theory. Relativity theory holds that there is no fixed space-time system as in Newtonian physics. The standard interpretation of quantum mechanics is that our knowledge of the most fundamental level of matter is strictly limited by the uncertainty principle, that events with no physical cause are pervasive in matter, and that nonlocality or action at a distance is also pervasive.

These developments in modern physics were quickly adopted by the new Romantic movement, since they seemed to support the main emphases of this movement. One of the first books was Fritjof Capra's book *The Tao of Physics* (1976), which argued that modern physics demonstrated the truth of Eastern mystical philosophy. This was followed by Gary Zukav's book *The Dancing Wu Li Masters* (1979) with a similar argument. More recently we have Danah Zohar's books *The Quantum Self: Human Nature and Consciousness Defined by the New Physics* (1990) and (with Ian Merchall) *The Quantum Society: Mind, Physics, and a New Social Vision* (1994). Most recently we have Diarmuid Ó Murchú's book *Quantum Theology: The Spiritual Implications of the New Physics* (1997), which explores these ideas further. All these works are examples of the current Romantic movement and its spin-off in the spirituality movement.

Finally, it should be made clear that the new Romantic and spirituality movements are not limited to the counterculture of the 1970s but continue into the present. I have mentioned above the work of Roof (1999), Fuller (2000), and Locklin (2005) on the baby boomers, those who grew up in the 1960s and 1970s. John R. Mabry, a researcher on Generation X (those born between the early 1960s and the early 1980s), states "Xers frequently equate 'religion' with hypocrisy, and prefer to speak of 'spirituality'." Furthermore, "Xers do have a myth: The Gnostic Myth."[45]

Now if it is the case that the phenomenon of "spiritual but not religious" is due in large part to the influence of the current Romantic move-

45. Mabry, "Gnostic Generation."

ment, then what does this mean for the spirituality movement? I believe that we need to assess the spirituality movement, affirm what is valid in it, and correct in it what we believe to be subversive of the Christian life. In particular, we should focus on the aspects of the spirituality movement that are derived from the influence of the current Romantic movement: an emphasis on interiority rather than the outer life of the body, community, and history; on individual and private life rather than public life; on feeling rather than rationality; and finally on spirituality rather than religion. I believe that Romantic movements are usually correct in their criticism of the cultural situation but dubious in their extremes and in some of their assumptions. For example, I would judge that the first Romantic movement was correct in its critique of the one-sidedness of the ideals of the Enlightenment and neoclassical traditions and the mechanical attitude of the emerging natural sciences toward the natural world. The Romantics attempted at least to restore a measure of balance by emphasizing the fundamental place of feeling, emotion, intuition, fantasy, and imagination in human life. But, of course, they went to extremes, since extremity was their middle name.

The same applies to the current Romantic movement. I believe that it is valid in its critique of the dominance of scientism, technology, industrialization, and consumerism and the resulting overrationalization, bureaucratization, and dehumanizing of society. But, as we have seen, in its extremity it often calls for a focus on interiority to the exclusion of the body and communal life, on private life to the exclusion of public life, on feeling to the exclusion of a balanced rationality, and on exotic spiritualities to the exclusion of the essential features of traditional religion.

However, their grounding in the perennial philosophy tradition is the most significant problem in one side of both Romantic movements, and the source of the main negative influence of the contemporary Romantic movement on the spirituality movement. The perennial philosophy is the religio-philosophical worldview exemplified by later Neoplatonism and Vedanta, and the philosophical foundations of Gnosticism, theosophy, and similar movements. I have noted above its influence on Novalis, Schopenhauer, Goethe, and Blake in the first Romantic movement. It has been propounded in the modern period by such philosophers as René Guénon, Frithjof Schuon, S. H. Nasr, and Huston Smith, among others. Roszak calls it the old Gnosis, which is exemplified in the hermetic tradition and Islamic, Jewish, and Hindu mysticism, that is, Sufism, Kabbalah, and Vedanta. As we have seen, Cyril O'Regan argues that Gnosticism has returned in German and English Romanticism, and thus that Romanticism is always based in part on the Gnostic tradition.

The perennial philosophy has influenced one side of the current Romantic and spirituality movements. The tendency of this worldview is to understand individuality or personhood as ambiguous, unreal, or evil. For example, Huston Smith states that in this worldview persons "sense themselves to be not finally real—*anatta*, no-self."[46] Also in this worldview bodily life and the natural world are viewed with suspicion; human communal life and history are seen to lack any meaning; and human fulfillment is found only in escape from the body and the world, and in a reunion of the human spirit, which is divine, with the divine itself.[47] The literary critic Harold Bloom, who calls himself a Gnostic, illustrates these points in his statement that we in the United States are "an obsessed society wholly in the grip of a dominant Gnosticism," which teaches a "knowledge, by and of an untreated self, or self-within-the-self, and the knowledge leads to freedom, a dangerous and doom-eager freedom: from nature, time, history, community, and other selves."[48] These views are contested by the other side of the current Romantic and spirituality movements, as they were also contested in the first Romantic movement by such figures as Schleiermacher and Coleridge. Also they are obviously in conflict with the tradition of biblical religion, which is the basis of the Christian life.

Thus I am suggesting that the spirituality movement should balance its emphasis on interiority with an equal concern with the outer life of the body, the community, and history. It should harmonize its emphasis on private individual life with an equal commitment to the importance of the public life of work and politics. And it should equalize its concern for feeling with an emphasis on the life of reason and reflection. In sum, it should balance its commitment to spirituality with an equal commitment to the life of religion with its concern for tradition, communal life, and involvement in public life. I agree with Sandra M. Schneiders, who, while implying that they are basically identical, has argued that religion and spirituality are "two dimensions of a single enterprise which . . .

46. H. Smith, *Forgotten Truth*, 52.

47. See Thomas, "Christianity and the Perennial Philosophy Philosophy," in Thomas, *What is it that Theologians Do?*

48. Bloom, *American Religion*, 49.

are essential to each other and constitute, together, a single reality" and "partners in the search for God," and that "religion is the optimal context for spirituality."[49]

49. Scnheiders, "Religion vs. Spirituality," 164–65, 176.

CHAPTER FOUR

Parish Ministry: A Theologian's Perspective

THE FUNDAMENTAL IMPORTANCE OF parish ministry today is that it is where the institutional church is located. It is where Christian people gather for public worship, preaching, sacraments, study, pastoral care, fellowship, and programs. It is where the organization and resources of the church are concentrated. It is where most clergy and lay leaders work. It is where the present opportunities for leadership are found. If we are to begin anew, therefore, to carry out the mission of the church, we must begin here in parish ministry.

Some very serious difficulties and dangers exist in parish ministry today, however, and these are the main focus of this essay. These problems, nevertheless, also point to the main opportunities in parish ministry.

The question with which to begin any reflection about the church and ministry concerns the mission of the church. Why is there a church? What is its purpose, its reason for being? What are Christians and the church supposed to be and do today? These are the fundamental questions of practical theology, of reflection on the practice of Christians and the church. These questions lie behind everything we are and do as Christians and the church. The answer that we give to this set of questions is—or ought to be—decisive for everything we do.

How then do we resolve such theological questions? The traditional Anglican norms for treating theological questions are scripture, tradition, reason, and experience. Innumerable books have been written on

51

the mission of the church on the basis of these norms.[1] The latter two norms, reason and experience, are especially important today because we are now in a cultural situation that is quite different from that of the first century CE and, indeed, of any century down to the last. Understanding the situation in which the church exists today, moreover, requires a good deal of social, economic, political, and cultural knowledge that is derived from reason and experience.

My understanding of the mission of the church, in summary, is that the church is to cooperate in God's mission in the world, the world that God created, loves, and wills to reconcile to God and lead to its fulfillment in God. Thus, the mission of the church is one of testimony, service, and action: testimony to God in Christ in word and deed, service to those in need, and action to fulfill God's will for justice and peace in the world. It has been said, therefore, that the church does not exist for the sake of itself but for the sake of the world. But, of course, the church is not simply instrumental, a means to an end. Because the church is a foretaste of the fulfillment, an end in itself, it can be a means of moving the world toward its fulfillment.[2]

In other words, the mission of the church is to be God's co-worker in the fulfillment of the divine purpose for the world, that is, salvation. We may define salvation as comprehensive well-being: physical, psychical, social, economic, political, cultural, and spiritual well-being, all based on the foundation of God's self-disclosure and the beginning of the fulfillment of the divine purpose in Christ. This understanding means that the mission of the church is primarily to the world, the whole world, and especially to that part of the world that is outside the church.

This view is clearly that of Scripture. God calls Abraham so that through his descendants all of the families of the earth will be blessed (Gen 12). The people of Israel are called to be a light to the nations so that God's salvation may reach to the ends of the earth (Isa 42:6–7, 49:6). In fulfillment of this vocation, Jesus is seen as a light to enlighten the Gentiles, the light of the world, and calls his followers to be the salt of the earth, the light of the world, and his witnesses to the end of the earth (Luke 2:32; John 8:12; Matt 5:13–16; Acts 2:8).

1. For my own view, see Thomas and Wondra, *Introduction to Theology*, chapter 17.
2. See, for example, Newbigin, *Household of God*, 168–70.

In light of this understanding of the mission and purpose of the church, it becomes clear that the main danger and difficulty confronting parish ministry today is that the residential parish, that is, the parish situated in a residential area—the predominant type of Christian congregation today—is in the worst possible position for carrying out this mission. The main reason for this is that the residential parish is almost entirely limited to and focused on the private life of its members, as distinct from their public life as workers and citizens. I believe this applies to most other parishes as well. Perhaps I exaggerate, caricature, and overlook exceptions, but I do so to make a point which I believe is largely valid.

Understanding this situation requires some history. Up until the nineteenth century, Western cultural life had a considerable unity. Family, social, economic, political, and religious life were usually fairly well-integrated and interdependent. Gibson Winter, a sociologist, described it in the following way.

> Residential community in this period coincided with economic, political, and cultural spheres of life; the household pattern of the village formed the hub for all community relationships. . . . The business of the world and the life of the congregation or parish took place in a common arena.[3]

In New England in the seventeenth century, for example, church and state were practically identical. Church membership conferred rights of citizenship. Congregational gatherings were the customary occasions for conducting elections, reading official proclamations, posting provincial laws, and conducting disciplinary hearings.[4] With the advent of the Industrial Revolution in the nineteenth century, all this changed, and the residential community became isolated from public life. Winter commented further.

> In the past century, the residential community has been segregated geographically, socially, and culturally from the economic and political structures of our society. This segregation of spheres of life in industrial society is the most important fact about social organization in the metropolis. . . . Perhaps more important than any other change has been the transformation of residential space into a reward for achievements in the economic enterprise; a high

3. Winter, *Suburban Captivity of the Churches*, 132.
4. Holifield, "Historian and the Congregation," 90–91.

salary enables one to choose a suitable neighborhood. Residence
has become the symbol of social position. Family problems, nurture of the young, neighborhood interests, informal association,
and general consumer activities fill the highly insulated sphere of
residential life
    . . . The sphere of residential activities is a very private aspect
of modern life.[5]

When this separation of private from public life occurred, the
church—without much conscious reflection—generally opted for private
residential life. This choice has apparently put it in the perfect position to
minister to the private and family lives of its members. (I shall comment
below about this term "apparently.") This choice, however, has also cut it
off for the most part from their public life, their economic and political
life, and their lives as workers and citizens. If the mission of the church
is to the world, especially the world outside the church, to public as well
as private life, then the church's option for residential life has tended to
undermine its ability to fulfill its mission.

Ever since the country's massive involvement in public life during
the New Deal and World War II, there has been a tendency on the part
of many in the United States to retire from public life into the calmer
satisfactions of family, recreation, and career. There was a partial return
of attention to public life in the civil rights and antiwar movements of the
1960s and early 1970s, and also more recently in the political activity of
the religious right. Generally, however, the "me" generation and the baby-
boomers have continued the tendency to retire to private life.

According to the Western tradition of philosophical and theological
thought, such a retreat is a diminishment of human life. From the emphasis in Greek thought on the life of the *polis* and in Roman thought on
the *res publica*, down through the centrality in Scripture and Augustine
of the reign of God and the city of God, participation in public life has
always been an essential dimension of human life. Any retirement from
it is an attenuation.

The classical liberal concepts of public and private refer generally to
social relations structured by the dimensions of access, agency, and interest. The story of religion in Western society in relation to the distinction
between public and private has been diverse and complex. Religion in

5. Winter, *Suburban Captivity*, 132–33. See also Jackson, *Crabgrass Frontier*.

the West has varied from being divided between public and private in Greece and Rome, to being an alternative to both—a third world—in medieval Christianity, to becoming something almost entirely public in the Reformation in Germany and England, and finally to something entirely private after the Enlightenment in classical liberalism. The option of the church for the private life, thus, has been reinforced by classical liberal ideology.

These concepts of public and private have been attacked in the past decade by certain critical theorists. They have pointed out that this distinction has been used by educated white males to restrict discussions of freedom, justice, and equality to the public realm and to relegate women and minorities to the private sphere where questions of freedom, justice, and equality are held to be irrelevant. They have also noted that the women's movement has begun to make what have hitherto been considered private matters into public issues, for example, reproductive freedom, domestic violence, care of the sick and elderly, and child care. These critiques have demonstrated the close interconnections of the public and private spheres, but they have not undercut the social and cultural significance of the distinction.[6]

The church, of course, does have a responsibility to minister to the private and family lives of its members through all of the activities of residential parish ministry that I have mentioned. This ministry, however, should essentially be one of Christian formation and preparation for the larger ministry of the church to the world, which I believe to be the heart of its mission. Moreover, because of the decisive impact of public life on private life, attending only to the private life of its members will undercut the effectiveness of the church's ministry to private life. For this reason I said above that the church's option for private life only "apparently" positioned it perfectly to minister to this area of life. One commentator has argued that preoccupation with private life and avoidance of public issues "fails to see the relationship between personal pain and public ill . . . We have known for some time, for example, that measures of family instability follow indices of economic hardship."[7]

6. See Thomas, "Public Theology and Counter-Public Spheres," and the references therein; especially see Benn, *Public and Private in Social Life,* 31–65 and 281–303. See also Benhabib, *Situating the Self,* 107–13.

7. Sample, *U. S. Lifestyles and Mainline Churches,* 118.

Furthermore, it is easy for the ministry of the church to the private and family lives of its members to be transformed gradually into an end in itself, one of institutional maintenance and survival, especially in a time of decline in membership and funds such as we see today. In such times we shall always begin to hear calls for programs of evangelism, education, and church growth to reverse the decline. Such programs will usually assume and be based on the residential parish system. It may well be, however, that the decline in church membership is ultimately the result of the failure of the church in its larger mission. Further programs based on the residential parish system are probably positioned least effectively for that mission. This situation is exactly what Winter predicted when he wrote in 1960 at the height of a great period of growth in the church: "Within a score of years, Protestantism will be fatally weakened as a significant religious force in the United Sates."[8] In other words, the church will be in decline because of failure in its larger mission.

The main reason for the claim that the church's option for private life has positioned it least effectively for its larger mission is that—in our contemporary society—private residential life is at the passive receiving end of society. It is not a particular form of private family and residential life that determines the nature of our economic, political, and cultural life, but rather just the opposite. It is in the public realm of economics and politics that the decisions are made that determine the character of our private life. Family residential life is concerned primarily with the consumption of the products of public life. This means that the residential parish system sits at the passive consuming end of our society rather than at the active and productive end.[9]

The nature of pastoral care and spiritual direction today provides an important example of this situation. It usually focuses entirely on the inner life, the emotional life, and the primary relationships of the family. Only very rarely, if ever, does it attend to issues deriving from public life, work, and citizenship. In this, as in many other ways, it is modeled on modern psychotherapy. In a recent study James Hillman, a distinguished Jungian analyst and author, stresses the catastrophic effects of this same tendency in psychotherapy. He claims that psychotherapy takes the

8. Winter, *Suburban Captivity*, 128.

9. My thesis here is very similar to that of Bellah et al., *Habits of the Heart*, esp. 167–95. (An updated edition with a new introduction was printed by the University of California Press in 1996.)

strong emotions of rage and fear, for example, which often derive from the public life of a person, and treats them only as problems of the inner life, as problems of personal growth, thus cutting them off from their relation to the larger community. This, he argues, has been a disaster for the public realm and for political life. Hillman states,

> There is a decline in political sense. No sensitivity to the real is-sues. Why are intelligent people—at least among the white middle class—so passive now? Why? Because the sensitive people are in therapy! They've been in therapy in the United States for thirty, forty years, and during that time there's been a tremendous politi-cal decline in this country. . . . Every time we try to deal with our outrage over the freeway, our misery over the office and the light-ing and the crappy furniture, the crime in the streets, whatever—every time we try to deal with that by going to therapy with our rage and fear, we're depriving the political world of something. And therapy, in its crazy way, by emphasizing the inner soul and ignoring the outer soul, supports the decline of the actual world. Yet therapy goes on blindly believing that it's curing the outer world by making better people. . . . It's not the case. . . .
>
> Do therapists ever ask their patients how they vote? . . . I asked that at a conference of therapists, and their answer was shock at the question.[10]

I am suggesting that an analogous phenomenon is happening in pastoral care and spiritual direction in the residential parish.

A closely related danger and problem of the residential parish sys-tem is that in American society today residential areas are the areas most thoroughly segregated by race, social class, economic status, and ethnic background.[11] In this situation the various programs of church growth tend to become what Winter calls "mission by co-optation," that is, the co-opting of new families of similar social and economic status.[12] Inviting people of quite different racial, economic, or ethnic backgrounds into a parish would produce disharmony, misunderstanding, mistrust, and strife. Since the purpose of the residential parish is often understood to be a haven from the strife and stress of the public world, then any source

---

10. Hillman, *We've Had a Hundred Years of Psychotherapy*, 5 and 216.

11. See Polenberg, *One Nation Divisible*.

12. Winter, *Suburban Captivity*, 71–76.

of disharmony would be seen as undercutting this purpose.[13] Thus a fundamental principle of the church growth movement is that the local church should be homogeneous. Anything else subverts church growth.

A preference for homogeneity in church life leads to the problem that David Kelsey calls "ideological distortion." He notes that the patterns of conduct and outlook of a given congregation are largely shaped by its social, economic, and political location in the larger society. He points out, however, that some congregations' patterns of conduct and outlook will be ideological in a second sense.

> These are congregations whose social location is determined by that population of the host society that benefits materially and in some (but not all) respects psychologically from unjust social, economic, and political structures by which other segments of the population are disempowered and oppressed.[14]

Insofar as the mission of the church involves the struggle for justice, such congregations—and there are many—will be very difficult places from which to begin.

Another danger and problem of residential parish ministry is clericalism, the privileging of clergy over laity and the identification of the church and the ideal Christian life with the clergy. Clericalism is a particular danger of the residential parish system because such a parish system focuses on corporate worship, preaching, sacraments, instruction, and pastoral care, all of which are the proper functions of the clergy. That is, the gathered community of the church is the main place where the clergy are called and prepared to function. Thus, the clergy and their functions are at the center of attention in the residential parish. The implicit message is that if you want to take the Christian life in the church seriously and actively, then you should model your life and activity on the clergy.

Moreover, since the clergy cannot carry on all of the ministry that needs to be done in the residential parish, they call on the laity to assist them in what they call lay ministry. To assist the clergy and to do

13. An excellent recent study, which brings Winter's thesis up to date, refers to this phenomenon as the "sanctuary orientation." See Roozen, *Varieties of Religious Presence*, 35–36, 254–57, and 177–216.

14. David H. Kelsey, "On the Congregation," in Hough, *Beyond Clericalism*, 18. I should point out that Kelsey is not a radical, "fire-eating" liberation theologian but the senior theologian at one of the most conservative of the large interdenominational university divinity schools.

the kind of work they do is thus considered to be the highest calling to which a lay person can aspire. This is clericalism. If, however, the mission of the church is not only the ministry to the private and family lives of the members of the church, but also and fundamentally the ministry of testimony, service, and action for the sake of the public life of the world, then clericalism—as I have described it—is undercutting the mission of the church.

Furthermore, the only people who are in a position to carry out the mission of the church in public life are lay people and not clergy since it is lay people who work forty hours a week or more in the economic, political, and cultural structures of the world. Lay people, not clergy, know firsthand the structures, processes, problems, and stresses of the public world, and therefore are in a position to address them as part of their ministry of testimony, service, and action. This work is what lay ministry should be about, but too often lay ministry is understood to mean helping the clergy. In this way clericalism is undercutting the mission of the church.[15]

A final danger and problem in residential parish ministry is that it is highly structured by gender. I have noted that residential life is largely private family life focused on intimate relationships, marriage, nurture of children, recreation, social life, and emotional health, all of which in a patriarchal society are considered stereotypically the feminine realm. This sphere of life is distinguished from the serious public, economic, and political realm where the really important decisions are made rationally by men—because it is the stereotypically male realm. Therefore, the area of life in which parish ministry is located is considered to be feminine, that is, passive, dependent, nonrational, and emotional. Thus, clergy are feminized, wear skirts, and play feminine roles in pastoral care, education, and the arrangement of the aesthetic aspects of worship. This is one reason why male clergy tend to spend a good deal of energy trying to prove that they are real men, regular fellows. Massive documentation for this situation can be found in Ann Douglas's book, *The Feminization of American Culture*, in which she analyzes the sentimentalization of

15. The classic statement of this understanding of the centrality of lay ministry in the mission of the church is Kraemer's *Theology of the Laity*. It is elaborated in Winter's *New Creation as Metropolis*. The most recent treatments are Rowthorn, *Liberation of the Laity*; and Thompsett, *We Are Theologians*.

American society—and especially religion—by Victorian clergymen and women authors.[16] Hers is a complex and fascinating thesis.

In a patriarchal society the feminine is generally perceived as subordinate, peripheral, marginal, less important, and requiring control. (This last attribute attests to a dark awareness in the patriarchal mind that the feminine is also mysterious, powerful, and dangerous, but to explore this awareness is beyond our present task.) In a patriarchal society all of these perceptions apply to the residential parish ministry as well, and any suggestion that the mission of the church has anything to do with the public male realm will meet strong resistance for fairly deep psychological reasons. Thus, patriarchal society and all of us within it will tend to be resistant to the mission of the church to public life for this reason, as well as for the fact that the church's mission will have to include the dismantling of its patriarchal character. Needless to say, this conclusion puts women clergy and lay leaders in a complex and difficult situation.

What I have depicted thus far is the external or cultural view of the gendered structure of the residential parish. There is, however, another side of this picture, namely, the internal, which is modeled on the larger society and is therefore patriarchal and hierarchical in character. At worst it can be a situation in which male clergy seek to dominate without competition. Being alone in the residential areas, primarily with women and children all week, they tend to develop a sort of extended household in which they can patronize, dominate, and occasionally abuse the women who work on the altar guild, in women's groups, and at parish suppers. When men occasionally do participate in church activities, it is usually in such stereotypically male activities as vestrymen, treasurers, or overseers of buildings and grounds. My point is that the highly gendered structure of the residential parish, both internally and externally, is a danger and a problem that is usually overlooked. The increasing participation of women in the public, economic, and political realm may be beginning to change this picture, but the stereotypes have deep roots and persist.

I have described some of the difficulties of residential parish ministry. As I said at the beginning, I may have exaggerated the situation and presented a caricature to which there are many exceptions.[17] I also said, however, that these dangers and problems point to the main opportunity

16. Douglas, *Feminization of American Culture.*
17. See, for example, Crabtree, *Empowering Church.*

of this ministry, namely, that the residential parish is where the church and its resources are concentrated. With the residential parish, therefore, we must begin.

Moreover, we must remember that "we believe in one holy catholic and apostolic Church." We believe that the Christians gathered in the residential parish are the people of God, the Body of Christ, the fellowship of the Holy Spirit, the community of hope, and participants in Christian salvation. They have received the gifts of faith, hope, love, joy, and peace, the gifts of grace for the work of ministry. We must remember that the one church is paradoxically both the motley group of sinners and the glorious company of the faithful. Because of this belief, we trust that the members of the residential parish will be looking for ways in which they can bring their faith and their gifts to bear on the pressing issues of public life today as they go about their lives in the public world.[18]

My main thesis about the mission of the church is that, while continuing and reforming its ministry to private residential life, the church must direct its attention to the world outside itself, the public world of economics and politics, because this public world is determinative of all the rest of life. Needless to say, undertaking this mission will involve fundamental systemic change in the church, and such change is extremely difficult to achieve.[19] The one person who has articulated this thesis most clearly and insistently is Gibson Winter, an Episcopal priest and sociologist who taught for many years at the University of Chicago. In two books published over thirty years ago, he mounted a massive critique of the residential parish system, and proposed a major revision of our understanding of the mission of the church, namely, the seeking of the reign of God through the creation of a humane metropolis. It is surprising that current literature on parish ministry, the congregation, and the mission of the church rarely refers to Winter's work.

Winter's proposal was that the goal of the church's mission should be the transformation of the metropolis. The metropolis is the main form in which the modern world exists, especially in the United States and Europe, but increasingly around the world. It is where most Americans live and where the major decisions are made that determine the character and quality of modern life. Winter's specific proposal took the form of

18. See Joseph C. Hough Jr., "Theologian at Work," in Dudley, *Building Effective Ministry*, esp. 130.

19. See Fenhagen, *Ministry for a New Time*, 86–109.

what he called sector ministries that organize slices of the metropolitan pie to include the contiguous parts of the concentric circles making up the metropolis. The goal is to open up communication and enable joint action for making the metropolis more humane.[20] I would expand his thesis to include more of the national and international arenas.

Winter's thesis, however, was just one proposal for the way in which the church can renew its mission to the public world. There have been many others. One of the first was Edward Ralph Wickham's *Church and People in an Industrial Society*.[21] Wickham was the founder of the Sheffield Industrial Mission in England, which became a model for similar projects in Detroit and Boston.[22] These and other similar efforts were costly; most of them did not survive when the finances of mainline denominations dwindled and attention turned to declining memberships. More recently, Martin Marty has proposed the model of the "public church," which is "especially sensitive to the *res publica*, the public order that surrounds and includes people of faith."[23]

The older model of the mission and ministry of the church in the public world is the chaplaincy in universities, hospitals, and prisons. The main problem with this older model is that it tended to focus on the private lives of the people in these institutions. That is, it took the form of a chaplaincy in the pejorative sense, namely, pastoral care and the blessing of the status quo without any critique of the structure and goals of the institution.

The first major difficulty that confronts any attempt to direct the mission of the church to the public world is the disunity of the church. The Christians present in any public institution, whether it be an industrial plant, a law firm, or a state legislature, are usually a cross-section of the denominational spread in that geographical area. Thus, the public mission of the church must be ecumenical or it will be hopelessly crippled. When the church is fulfilling its proper mission, the disunity of the church will be seen as an intolerable outrage. Indeed, the modern ecumenical movement was born in the mission fields of Asia and in

20. Winter, *Suburban Captivity*, 129–59.

21. Wickham, *Church and People in an Industrial City*.

22. See Paradise, *Detroit Industrial Mission*. For a description of efforts in the 1960s to get congregations to attend to their mission to public life, see Reitz, *Church in Experiment*.

23. Marty, *Public Church*, 3.

the universities of Western Europe. In the residential parish system the disunity of the church is hardly noticed, let alone seen to be an intolerable outrage. This observation can be interpreted to indicate that the church there is not pursuing its primary mission. In the residential setting there is apparently no necessity for the churches to cooperate except for lack of funds. In the various public settings it *is* a necessity.

One way to begin to think about reforming the mission of the church in the residential parish setting is for the congregation to ask itself such questions as these: What are the main dangers to the purposes of God in this place? Are they unemployment, racism, drugs, sexism, exploitation of workers, housing discrimination, pollution of the environment, crime, or what? How are these issues related to the larger social, economic, political, and cultural structures of the nation and the world? What access do we have to these issues and structures? What resources do we have for this access? Where can we start? With whom can we fruitfully cooperate? It is clear from these questions, moreover, that the main leaders and workers in the mission of the church in relation to these issues will have to be lay people.

In a parish in which I worked sixty years ago, there were seventy-five physicians on the rolls. To my knowledge, however, nothing was ever done to recognize this fact or to gather the physicians together to discuss their common problems from a Christian point of view or, for example, the issue of the delivery of health care in the Boston area. An opportunity was lost.

The final area of reform in the mission of the church in the residential parish is Christian education concerning the political responsibility and participation of all members at the municipal, state, national, and international levels. Since most of the problems we face as a nation cannot be resolved by individual action, the commandment to love our neighbors near and far sends us into politics. There is often education in parishes about national problems, such as the environment, drugs, and homelessness, and there are often proposals for involvement in local service in regard to these issues. Only very rarely, if ever, is there instruction with regard to our access as citizens to the structural and systemic causes of these problems through the total electoral process of finding good candidates, campaigning, voting, and guiding elected or appointed officials. Since the Vietnam War and Watergate, concerned church members have often been alienated from the political process. They have been drawn instead to what I call movement politics, which tends to ignore electoral politics and thus has little effect on the issues at hand.[24]

If the problems of residential parish ministry appear huge, if the possibilities of meeting them often seem difficult and remote, there are fundamental grounds for hope. When the people of God gather for the preaching of the Word and the celebration of the sacraments, for study and service, for fellowship and rejoicing, then we believe that God in Christ through the Spirit is present among them giving them insight and empowering them to seek the divine will in their lives in families and in the public world. With this hope all things are possible.[25]

24. See Appendix to chapter 9.

25. This chapter is based on a lecture originally delivered in September 1989 in the basic course in the Parish Ministry in the Contemporary World Program at the Episcopal Divinity School under the direction of the late Rev. Dr. George Hunter. I should note that my qualifications for speaking on this topic are somewhat slim. I have worked part-time in about fifteen parishes in the dioceses of Washington, New York, Massachusetts, and New Hampshire. I have also been in charge of a couple of parishes, but never the rector.

CHAPTER FIVE

A Parish Story

I AM THE RECTOR of St. Paul's Church, Middletown. It is an unusual parish and that is what this story is about. Seven years ago there was a fire, and the church, the parish house, and the rectory, which were all connected, burned to the ground. My elderly predecessor, whose main accomplishment had been the erection of these buildings, was so stricken by the blow that he felt he should resign and retire. So I was called to be the rector of a parish that owned some land but no other property. I had a vague idea that this situation might offer the parish an opportunity for a new beginning, but I had not thought very much about it.

I will never forget the first vestry meeting. I really had no special plan in mind and had no idea of what was about to happen. After the usual amenities of welcoming the new rector, the first order of business was the plans for the building of a new, larger, and finer St. Paul's. Apparently a committee had been at work on this for some time and had drawn up rough plans and an estimate of the cost. For some reason I had not been told about this committee and was rather miffed that I had not been consulted. But there they were: new plans and architect's drawings for a new church, parish house, and rectory with all the latest equipment. The bill was rather staggering, $5 million, which would mean a very heavy mortgage.

As the discussion proceeded, I could see that there was great enthusiasm and zeal for the whole idea. However, a picture in my mind was troubling me. I recalled the first time I had walked around the blackened ruins of St. Paul's. The thing that struck me was that as I looked around I could see five other churches, most of them with large parish houses within a few blocks of St. Paul's. So at the next pause in the lively discussion of the new plans, I said, "Why do you want to build a new church? There are five other churches within sight of St. Paul's."

There was an electric silence, a couple of gasps of incredulity, and then general laughter at what was taken to be a good joke. But when they realized that I seemed to be serious, many of the vestry got quite angry. Did I mean that St. Paul's should just fold up and go out of business? Why, the very idea! Why, my grandfather was a founder of St. Paul's church. Middletown needs St. Paul's. What would other churches think? What would the bishop think? And so forth.

After being pushed around a bit, I began to realize that what I had blurted out might really have some possibilities. I pointed out that within four blocks of St. Paul's were five other large churches with well-equipped parish halls, and that any businessman who suggested the expenditure of $5 million for the duplication of such buildings would be fired. I knew the analogy was not a very good one, but I couldn't think of a better one at the moment. After tempers had cooled and we had apologized for being so sharp in our comments, we began to discuss the real issue in earnest.

This was the first of many long discussions and debates in the vestry that extended over six months. Two members resigned in a huff saying that they were going to the bishop to get a new parish started with a new rector who had some sense. Some of the vestry were intrigued with the idea that it was not absolutely necessary to have new buildings. A couple of the vestry seized on the idea almost from the beginning and carried most of the debate themselves. They said, "Middletown doesn't need any more church buildings. We can use the other churches around here. The church really is not buildings anyway. It is rather a community of Christians."

So the argument raged back and forth and soon the whole parish was involved. The vestry held several open meetings in the auditorium of the junior high school across the street to discuss the question of whether or not to rebuild. I was very impressed with how articulate some of the vestry were who were questioning the rebuilding plan. They had obviously been doing some serious thinking and even reading on the nature of the church and its mission. They pointed out, for example, that Jesus had directed his disciples to travel light, apparently a reference to Matt

10:9–10, and that the early church had never erected any buildings for public worship for over three hundred years. On the other hand, the feelings favoring rebuilding were strong and were expressed with passion. We had obviously touched on a deep psychological nerve in the parish that was closely tied up with self-image and social standing. As a friend of mine had put it, "In the church the Oedipus complex is outrun only by the edifice complex." Not having fine, beautiful, well-equipped buildings was rather like not having fine clothes. It was embarrassing and something to be ashamed of. As clothes make the man, so buildings make the church. In fact they *are* the church.

So at the end of six months I was surprised to realize that the vestry had actually come to a decision not to rebuild. It was not as clear-cut as that, and the decision had seemed to emerge more as a sort of unconscious but unchallenged assumption that, in fact, we were not going to rebuild. For some who were not really convinced, this was understood to mean that we were not going to rebuild for the time being.

In the meantime, St. Paul's had been conducting a Eucharist at 9:30 a.m. on Sundays at the nearby Presbyterian church, and it was decided to continue this indefinitely. The Presbyterians wanted to offer us the use of their buildings free of charge, assuming that this was a temporary arrangement while we built a new church. They insisted loudly that they were very glad to help out their Christian brothers and sisters in their time of need. I thought I detected a note of condescension in their heartiness, but that was probably the creation of my suspicious mind. I raised the question of paying rent to the Presbyterians with the vestry, and after some debate the vestry decided to do this and make it clear to them that we had no plans to rebuild. The Presbyterians received this with some incredulity but finally agreed, mentioning the fact that they could barely afford the expenses of upkeep along with payments on their mortgage.

St. Paul's had a tradition of an 8:00 a.m. Eucharist, followed by family service of Morning Prayer at 9:00 a.m., and then a choral Eucharist at 11:00 a.m. Because this was no longer possible, the vestry after some discussion decided to combine these services into one including Morning Prayer, sermon, and Eucharist with hymns in between so that people could come to any part or combination they chose. I was surprised by the number of people who at first came for only the sermon. I discovered that many of them were in fact inquirers who wanted to find out something about Christian faith and life and how it was possible in the modern world. They were not ready for Christian worship. Gradually several of this group began to attend the first two parts and later all three. Also, a sort of continuous coffee hour was held in the parish hall from about 9:00 a.m. to 11:00 a.m., at which the debate over rebuilding and related issues was carried on. Since all the *Prayer Books* and Hymnals had been destroyed in the fire, I suggested that each family buy these and bring them to church. Also, I began to conceive the possibility of a parish that did not own any property at all.

The next big problem was the church school. The Presbyterians used their church school rooms most of Sunday mornings so that they were not available to us. This gave me the opportunity to raise another earth-shaking question. This time, however, I had thought it through beforehand and didn't blunder into it the way I had with the question of rebuilding. When the question first came up in the vestry, I asked, "Why do you want a church school anyway?" Although the vestry should have been prepared for this kind of question from me, it received the same flood of answers as rebuilding. "Why St. Paul's has always had one of the finest church schools in Middletown. Over one hundred and fifty children wasn't it? Are we going to let our children grow up without any education in Christianity?"

After the first barrage I said that in my experience, church schools as they now existed, really amounted to not much more than a sitting service so that the parents could have a little peace and quiet after a late Saturday night. I know that was probably a serious exaggeration, but I wanted to raise the issue sharply. This produced another long debate that overlapped with that of rebuilding and ran for several weeks. The course of the discussion and division of opinion were similar to the debate about rebuilding. It ran something like this:

"Why do you want a church school?"

"To educate our children about Christianity."

"Can't *you* do that?"

"Well, I suppose we could, but the church school teachers are much better equipped."

"But some of you are church school teachers. Are you better equipped than the other parents?"

"Mm, well, I guess not."

"'Then why don't you do it at home at your own convenience without the weekly convulsion of getting the children out at 9:00 a.m. on Sundays?'"

"But wouldn't that involve a lot of duplication of effort? Also our children are of different ages and we would have to teach them separately."

"Then why don't you do some exchanging so that you would have only one age group?"

"But we don't know enough to do it well."

"I would be very glad to help you in any way I can."

Long silence. Mixed reactions. Some agreeing, some mumbling disagreement. Again, I discovered that one of the main problems was losing face in the community. It was pointed out that the Methodists had a huge magnificent church school with two hundred children in two shifts, with the latest equipment, movie and DVD projectors, and so forth.

The debate went on so long that the church school was dropped by default the first year. The fact that all the records and materials had been destroyed in the fire made this a little easier. Also, the people were surprised and somewhat embarrassed at the loud and happy reaction of the children. And some of the regular church school teachers privately expressed a sense of relief. The debate continued through the first year. And I began to realize that there would probably not be a church school the second year either. The vestry didn't want to admit it, but it seemed clear that many were relieved by the absence of the church school.

To make a long story somewhat shorter, after two years of no organized church school, I discovered that certain earnest parents had quietly begun to instruct their own children at home and that some had arranged exchanges with other parents. Some did it in the evenings and some on Saturday mornings. These informal arrangements grew slowly, and I came to know about them when some parents came to me for help. I had to spend a great deal of time examining various church school materials that might be of use to the parents. I also spent a lot of time with the parents who were doing the teaching, and in many cases this led to lengthy discussions about their questions and problems. Gradually this became more regularized, and by the end of the third year I was meeting one evening a week with groups of parents involved in teaching children of different age groups. A Bible class for parents and others developed and also shorter term groups on sex education, drug addiction, and other issues.

Because I didn't know much about educational methods for children, I inquired and got the names of some of the better teachers in the public schools and persuaded them to help in consulting with the parents who were teaching. I insisted that, much to the surprise of the vestry and the parents, these teachers receive a consulting fee of $50 per hour. This had the beneficial effect on the teachers of pride in their expertise, causing them to be better prepared, and helping the parents to take the whole business more seriously.

Some parents, after trying for a while, finally decided that they couldn't do a very good job instructing their own children. So I helped them to find someone in the parish who was willing and able to do this. Again, I insisted that they be paid $75 per week. At first this was greeted with disbelief. What? Pay church school teachers? Ridiculous! Why, my aunt so-and-so taught in the church school for forty years and never received a cent for it! I resisted the temptation to comment on this.

This time, the debate did not last so long, and within a few months we had about a half dozen classes being conducted by paid teachers meeting at different times during the week. Again, the financial commitment paid off. All involved took the classes more seriously. Within a year most of the classes had gravitated to Saturday morning. Because most of them wanted more space and quieter surroundings, at my suggestion, the vestry arranged with the Middletown School Committee to rent the first floor rooms of the junior high school building across the street for two hours on Saturday mornings. As one vestryman put it, "I have always thought it was rather ridiculous to have our church school rooms empty all week while the public school rooms were empty all weekend."

This brings me to the last of the buildings destroyed in the fire, the rectory. When I arrived the vestry had rented a house for me and my family, but were, of course, planning to build a new rectory next to the new church and parish house. Much to my surprise, after deciding not to rebuild the church or parish house, they were still planning to build a new rectory whereas I had assumed that their negative decision about the other buildings included the rectory. I told the vestry that I and my family preferred not to live in a rectory owned by the church. The vestry were quite taken back, and asked me to explain. So I told them the long, sad story about living in the church-owned rectory of my previous parish.

I explained that the members of my former parish had considered the rectory to be a sort of annex of the parish house next door. That is, they considered it their property, which it was, but they also considered it public property, which it was not. We had very little privacy. Parishioners would walk in day and night sometimes without even knocking. They often seemed insulted if the door was locked or they received less than a warm welcome from me or my wife. They also seemed to assume that the rectory was a combination short-order restaurant and bar. Breakfasts, coffee breaks, lunch, tea, cocktails, supper, nightcaps. We seemed to be holding a continuous open house. All this reminded me of the comment of a seminary classmate who, after his first year in a parish, commented, "Now I understand why I studied Greek in seminary; I'm in the restaurant business!"

Another problem was that the members of the parish insisted on decorating the rectory according to their own tastes, or, as my wife would say, lack of taste. The result was what my wife called a combination of neo-Sears Roebuck and free association. They also insisted on furnishing it in part, and seemed surprised, if not offended, when we politely declined some of the furniture that they had retrieved from their attics.

The parishioners, however, were very good about upkeep and repairs. Some of them were carpenters, painters, and plumbers who insisted on doing the work themselves on off hours, usually early in the morning or at night. They, too, often walked in without knocking and seemed to expect coffee or a beer. They refused to be paid for their labors, but the work often did not get done for months. I also discovered that the church-owned rectory was in the minds of my former vestry the justification for my salary of $40,000, which was about half of the average salary of the members of the parish.

Another point in my sad story is that the church-owned rectory cut me off from the community. I paid no property taxes and thus tended not to get involved in various city problems in regard to schools, zoning, sewers, trash collection, and so forth. I had the feeling of being kept and protected from life of the town.

I also discovered that because of my low salary, the members of the parish tended, probably unconsciously, to take a patronizing or paternalistic attitude toward me and my family. We were the object of charity. One wealthy couple wanted to give us a membership in the country club. Another invited us to use their summer place on the lake, another their winter place in Florida, all in the off-season, of course. To all these kind offers, and with a willpower unusual for me, I gave them a polite but firm refusal with the very subtle hint, which became less and less subtle as the years went by, that if they were really feeling generous, they could raise my salary so that we could afford these things ourselves.

Throughout all this discussion and in my recollections of my previous parish, I slowly became aware of an unconscious assumption that the clergy ought to be poor, perhaps to keep them honest, or so that they could be kept in their place by patronizing gifts, or perhaps so that there would be at least one example in the parish of a family espousing Christian poverty. Maybe I was all wrong in this psychologizing, for they were honest and generous people. But it seemed to be that we were up against some deeply buried stereotype about the life of the clergy.

My long sad story had been delivered with more emotion than I had planned, and it was met with an embarrassed silence. I, too, became embarrassed, because it suddenly occurred to me that some aspects of my story had been true of my predecessor at St. Paul's.

There were some questions and discussion, but it was much shorter than that about the other buildings. After two meetings the vestry agreed to raise my salary by an amount equivalent to the rental, upkeep, utilities, taxes, on the house we were living at the present. This turned out to be considerably less than the cost of building a new rectory and paying on a mortgage. They were rather surprised, however, to discover that this added up to a salary of $60,000 which was almost the equivalent of some of theirs.

The result was that after the first year, my wife and I bought a house about a mile from the church, decorated and furnished it ourselves and never again were bothered by possessive parishioners. The first couple of years, however, we went out of our way to invite to our house as many of the members of the parish as we could, and they seemed very pleased to be invited.

There is one final part of my story about the buildings. My office was not at home. I am the father of a rather loud family who came to have many friends who are regularly phoning and ringing the doorbell. So I could not work at home. At first there were murmurs about the rector having his study in his "home." I tried to explain gently that this was probably a hangover from an age of governesses and servants that was long gone, at least for the clergy.

The upshot was that I rented an office in a downtown office building occupied by business people, lawyers, doctors, architects, and other professionals. In this setting there was not much argument when I insisted on hiring my own secretary and buying my own office equipment. Since these expenses were usually born by the church, the vestry voted to increase my salary to $80,000 a year.

When some of the members of the parish complained that this was an unconscionably high salary to pay a rector, especially when compared the salaries of other clergy in the city, the vestry were quick to point out that the parish budget was only one third of what it had been in the past. The total budget consisted of my salary, rental to the Presbyterian church, salaries for church school teachers and teaching consultants, plus the diocesan assessment. This all amounted to about $200,000 per year whereas in the years before the fire it amounted to about $600,000. The difference was that the insurance paid off the mortgage, and there were no expenses for upkeep, janitorial services, repairs, and utilities.

Many parishioners thought that there must be something wrong in a parish with such a low budget. This seemed to be connected with their ecclesiastical self-image and standing in the community. This size of a budget seemed to put them in the same category with the Pentecostal chapel on the edge of the city. One canny member of the vestry suggested that there might have been something wrong with the previous system with its very large budget. Some of the vestry wondered out loud whether such a low budget would elicit the same level of commitment to the parish as in the past. One of the most thoughtful vestry members who had been most intrigued by the new developments at St. Paul's and who had done some thinking about the mission of the church had an interesting answer to these questions. She said, "Look, there are plenty of problems in Middletown that need the attention, concern, and financial commitment of Christians. Being relieved of the burden of all the buildings frees us to turn our attention to where it really belongs as Christians, namely, to the people and problems in this city that need our help."

This led to further discussions about the responsibility of the people of St. Paul's for the city at large. Over the years this led to many projects initiated by members of St. Paul's: the youth drop-in center, the jail-visiting project and the half-way house, the drug-addiction clinic, the low cost housing committee, and the political issues forum. These came to involve other churches under the guidance of the Middletown Ecumenical Association.

One interesting sidelight to this was the gradual dissolution of many of the parish organizations of St. Paul's: the Episcopal Youth group, the Episcopal Church Women, the Men's Club, the young adults association, the usual roster. I am not sure I understand why this happened, and I don't think I was trying to undercut them. The only clue I can think of is that these organizations were somehow associated with the buildings of St. Paul's, perhaps with the sense that they ought to be used or at least appear to be used. When the buildings were gone and it became clear that there was to be no pressure to raise money to build new ones, most of the organizations tended to peter out.

The other reason for the disappearance of most of the organizations was the fact that their members began to be drawn into the various projects outside of the parish. The youth group took over the youth center. The Men's Club ran the jail-visiting program and the half-way house. The Episcopal Church Women became the staff of the drug addiction center and so forth. Since these also became ecumenical ventures, the St. Paul's groups became less visible. I think that some of the original organizations continued to meet, and they tended to meet for purely social purposes. They liked to get together, and I agreed that this is the best reason of all.

My story is about at an end. It is not the end of the story of St. Paul's. I have not told of our other ecumenical ventures, first with the Presbyterians in worship, the church school, certain community projects, and later with other churches. We learned that buildings seemed to be the main barrier to ecumenical cooperation—something that had not occurred to us before. I have not said anything about how the team ministry grew up in our area of Middletown. I have not told of the reaction of other churches to our decision not to rebuild, nor of the weird problems we had with the Bishop in this connection. I have not told how we finally sold the land and invested in a low cost housing project. Somehow, all these things grew out of that fire.

The most important development for me that came out of all this is the transformation that occurred in the understanding of my ministry both for me and for the people of St. Paul's. This is rather difficult to describe. One way to put it is that besides being the main minister of the Word and the sacraments, I have become a sort of an adviser or consultant to St. Paul's. I spend a great deal of time in my office talking with St. Paul's people not only as a pastoral counselor, but also as an adviser on projects, a consultant on a wide range of problems that emerge in urban life today. The fact that my office is downtown has seemed to indicate that I am concerned about issues in the public lives of St. Paul's people as much with the problems of their private and family lives. For the same reason I spend a lot of time with people who have nothing to do with St. Paul's including members of the City Council and the School Committee and other civic groups. Sometimes I get the impression that many people take me to be some sort of a consultant on ethical, strategic, and occasionally theological issues. I don't charge fees for this, but I have considered doing that. I once inquired about this at a vestry meeting. Some of the vestry expressed doubt about this aspect of my work. One said, "You are *our* minister and we expect you to minister primarily to us." This was countered by another member who said, "That's true. He *is* supposed to minister to us, but *we* are supposed to minister to Middletown. So part of his ministry to us is to represent and model for us a ministry to Middletown." In the ensuing discussion I got the impression this expressed the consensus of the vestry.

This, however, is a rather demanding and frightening kind of role to play, something I was hardly prepared for in seminary. The result is that I have to spend a good deal of time reading books, journals, magazines, and reports of various kinds. The outer room of my office has become a small theological library, which has branched out into the literature on all the social, political, and cultural problems of our day.

This worried some people in the parish. A vestry member once took me aside to say that he thought I ought to spend less time reading books and more time calling on the parishioners. We talked about this for quite a while. I tried to explain that I always called on parishioners who were sick or in some kind of crisis, but that I couldn't call on all the members regularly even if I spent full time on it. I also reminded him that I had trained a group of parishioners to do some of the calling and mentioned that some of them were more experienced in counseling people in certain situations than I was. I went on to explain that the purpose of the church and the responsibility of its members was very problematic in a time of rapid social and economic change, and that it required a great deal of careful study, reflection, and conversation to get clear on the meaning and implications of Christian faith and life in the modern world.

One of the main insights I have gained from the story of St. Paul's is the significance of money and paying people for their work. This has really transformed the church school. Also, the size of my salary seems to have brought about a fundamental change in the parish's attitude toward me and its understanding of my ministry. All patronizing seems to have disappeared. Also, people seem freer to make demands on my time.

Probably the most striking result of that fire in the long run has been the great change that has slowly taken place in people's understanding of the church and of St. Paul's parish in particular. The fundamental source is that now St. Paul's church does not own a nickel's worth of property. Everyone realizes that this is in a sense a parasitical situation, that we do need and use buildings that are owned and maintained by other people. You cannot imagine, however, what this means for the members of St. Paul's. In a way it disembodies the meaning of the church, but it also embodies it in a new way.

One thoughtful woman put it this way:

> Before the fire whenever someone mentioned St. Paul's church, I always thought of those beautiful old buildings that I had known so well all my life. I thought of the services and the meetings we held in them, the joyful occasions and the sad. But now when someone mentions St. Paul's I don't think of the buildings any-more. And it is not the Presbyterian church that comes to mind. It is rather certain people who come into my mind's eye, usually those I had most recently seen and talked with at the last service or at the last meeting or at the clinic. So the image I have of the church is sort of a mobile and changing thing, groups of people doing things together, on the move.

She was silent a moment and then continued:

> I think we have lost something in not having buildings anymore. But maybe that's just nostalgia and longing for the good old days, so called. Maybe what we have lost is a sense of safety, security and belonging, a place. But perhaps God doesn't want us to have that kind of security today. We've lost something, but I know we have gained something, too. It's hard to put it exactly. I guess it's just a clearer picture of what the church is all about. Somehow those wonderful old buildings got in the way of that.

Again a period of silence, and then she said, "It was quite a fire."

CHAPTER SIX

The Poverty of Preaching in the Episcopal Church

I BELIEVE THAT PREACHING in the Episcopal Church is generally poor. By that I mean simply that there is a general failure to preach the gospel of the good news of God in Christ. A former dean of King's College, Cambridge, put it this way in commenting on preaching in the Episcopal Church in the twentieth century:

> But what shook me most of all is the character of the preaching that seems to prevail in your churches. . . . Preachers take texts from Scripture (though they do not always do that), and treat them as mottoes or captions under which they excogitate some religious or moral lessons that have little, if any, direct relation to the Scripture they have quoted. Who preaches sermons that are genuine expositions of the text and sense of Scripture, bringing to bear the great biblical themes of God's judgment and mercy upon men who are dead in their complacency, self-confidence or pride? Your preachers are still advocating justification by works of one kind or another (they may be very orthodox or very Catholic works); they are not preaching the gospel of salvation by faith in Jesus Christ.[1]

I am convinced that this assessment was, and still is, correct. It is confirmed by my own impressions, gained over sixty years of extended experience in six dioceses from Georgia to New Hampshire and from New York to California, and occasional experience in several others. Needless

1. Vidler, *Essays in Liberality*.

to say there have been some glowing exceptions, some experiences of excellent preaching. These, however, have only sharpened the contrast and the general impression of widespread poverty. My experience and judgment have also been confirmed by those of others. It was for me a striking testimony that the first general secretary of the World Council of Churches stated that the main thing that Anglicanism and the Episcopal Church could learn from the ecumenical church was preaching. He said that he believed that preaching was the weakest element in our life as a church. He cited an example from his recent attendance at an Anglican cathedral, adding that it was not an isolated experience for him and his colleagues at the World Council as they traveled around the world and the Anglican Communion, including the Episcopal Church.

More recent evidence concerning the state of preaching in the Episcopal Church can be found in the essays that celebrated the fiftieth anniversary of the College of Preachers, essays on preaching and the teaching of preaching in the Episcopal Church.[2] The warden of the College expressed the consensus of these essays in this way:

> Preaching [in the Episcopal Church] is usually not done well; on that there is general agreement. It is often boring, devoid of creative reflection, and in any other setting than the liturgy might constitute a major threat to the survival of religion. Sermons are often composed by overworked clergy in hasty desperation because time has run out, and sound like it. They lean heavily on truisms and repeat endlessly the obvious and the familiar. . . . Congregations return with indomitable hope to the hearing of mediocre preaching.[3]

In this essay, I will suggest that a major cause of this is the general failure to address the theology of preaching in the Episcopal seminaries, and I will offer some evidence of this failure. I will then suggest that this situation has deeper roots in the Anglican tradition (and the Catholic tradition generally). I will go on to propose that the solution to this problem lies in becoming clearer on the theology of preaching. Finally, I will outline an argument from Scripture, tradition, and reason for one view of

2. The essays, several of which are referred to in the following footnote, appeared in the July 1980 issue of *Anglican Theological Review*.

3. Welsh, "Preaching as Apologetics," 239–40; see also Evans, "Introduction," 195; Snow, "Reflections on Anglican Preaching," 211; and Nichols, "What is the Matter with the Teaching of Preaching?" 221–22 and 234.

the theology of preaching and also what this implies for the preparation of sermons.

∽

What, then, accounts for the situation I have alleged to exist—the poverty of preaching in the Episcopal Church? I believe that neglect of the theology of preaching is a major cause. By the theology of preaching I do not mean the theology *in* preaching, the relation of Christian doctrine to preaching. I mean the relation of *God* to preaching. It is commonly agreed that a theological question is a question about God or about God's relation to the world or some aspect of the world. For example, this is the immediate implication of Paul Tillich's two formal criteria of theology, which distinguish it from other intellectual endeavors, whether in the humanities or the natural and human sciences.[4] The theology of preaching will therefore be concerned with this question: What do we hope and expect to happen between God and the congregation in preaching? I believe that our answer to this question will in large part determine how we preach.

My claim is not that the poverty of preaching in the Episcopal Church is *solely* a matter of theology. For one thing, de-emphasis of preaching is a general phenomenon in American churches. The sociologist of religion David Roozen describes what he calls "the most profound mega-trend" in contemporary American religion as a shift from "Word to Spirit," which he characterizes as a shift from an emphasis on expository preaching to a more experiential and subjective emphasis.[5] Furthermore, important aspects of our contemporary cultural situation tend to downgrade the significance of preaching. These include the current Romantic movement with its emphasis on feeling and the non-verbal,[6] the dominance of the new electronic media over linear verbal discourse, and the focus of these media on entertainment, such that the value of preaching is taken to be its entertainment value. Finally, a class phenomenon may be relevant

4. See Tillich, *Systematic Theology*, 1:11–15; see also Aquinas *Summa Theologiae* Ia, 1, 7.

5. See website <hirr.hartsem.edu>: Hartford Institute for Religious Research, Roozen lecture, 2001.

6. See, for example, Roszak, *Where the Wasteland Ends*; and Fleischner, *Auschwitz, Beginning of a New Era? Reflections on the Holocaust*, pt. 7: "The New Romanticism and Biblical Faith."

here. Episcopalians may tend to think that evangelical, exegetical preaching is "not for people like us but rather for those other people who attend Baptist and Pentecostal churches and who like and need this kind of preaching, whereas we prefer a more intellectual type of preaching"—referring, perhaps without realizing it, to the style of Anglican preaching of the eighteenth century marked by classical rhetorical elegance and learned allusion.

But even when all this is granted, the theology of preaching remains an important and indeed a decisive question, and over the years I have formed the impression that it is a question rarely treated in the homiletics courses in Episcopal seminaries. Apparently it is assumed that the theology of preaching is not a topic worth addressing. One commentator on the teaching of homiletics in Episcopal seminaries stated in the issue of this journal mentioned above: "A major weakness of our teaching is a *theological* uncertainty at the core of the content of preaching: What do we do with something like the Word that claims to be transcendent yet appears in so human a symbolic form? . . . Episcopalians run from it."[7]

In order to assess whether this theological uncertainty is being dealt with, twice over a period of five months in the spring and summer of 2002 I wrote to the professors of homiletics at the eleven Episcopal seminaries. I requested the syllabi of their courses, and received responses from eight of them.[8] At least one course in homiletics is required for the MDiv degree at all but one of the eight schools. I examined the syllabi that I received and read the assigned reading for each of eleven courses. I read many excellent books on various aspects of preaching: on structure, presentation, the use of story, image, and metaphor; on types and styles of preaching (narrative, topical, inductive, conversational, African American, evangelistic, expository, devotional, pastoral, biblical, imaginative, phenomenological); on images of the preacher: herald, pastor, storyteller, witness, and so forth. A few of these books mention the theology of preaching in passing. Only one addresses it at any length. Richard Lischer, a leading homiletician, laments that "the many books on form

---

7. Nichols, "What is the Matter with the Teaching of Preaching?" 234–35.

8. The professors at three of the seminaries are from other schools or local parishes and are not Episcopalians. Is this fact indicative of the status accorded to preaching in these seminaries, or a lack of able Episcopal mentors? Either way, it is not encouraging.

and design which have dominated our generation's homiletical thinking cannot produce the renewal promised by the gospel."[9]

In addition to what I learned from the readings assigned in the courses, I discovered that the theology of preaching was an explicit topic in only three of them. When I inquired further about these, I discovered that the theology of preaching is usually understood to mean the place of doctrine in preaching. For example, the topic in one class was described as "Preaching theology, i. e. preaching on the teachings of the Church. Your preaching of your own theology. . . . To consider how topical sermons on theological subjects are necessary and appropriate for a congregation's annual round of sermons." In the instructions for an assigned paper on the theology of preaching, another professor said that it was a matter of identifying the doctrine preached in a sermon. This understanding was supported by one of the assigned texts, which states that one of the important steps in creating a sermon is to choose a doctrine arising from the theme of the sermon.[10] In another assigned text the author states that the aim of his book is to "show how theology informs preaching," but this is interpreted to mean "preaching as the final form of theology."[11]

On the other hand, several of the assigned readings imply or refer in passing to the theology of preaching—in the sense in which I defined it above—usually in the form of the word of God or revelation. But this is only rarely elaborated or emphasized. Only one of the assigned texts has a clear and strong statement of the theology of preaching, very similar to the one I will outline below. It is limited, however, to ten pages at the end of a 460-page text.[12] And in the one course in which this text is required, the whole book is discussed in two hours. Although two of the seminaries emphasize expository, evangelical preaching, interpreted as the Word of God, it is not clear how this theology is elaborated. One of the courses I investigated includes a fine, thorough analysis of the steps involved in exegesis.

My survey of the teaching of homiletics in the Episcopal seminaries is obviously not exhaustive, and it may be that the theology of preaching as defined is treated more often and more fully than I was able to deter-

9. Lischer, *Theories of Preaching*, 2.

10. See Wilson, *Four Pages of a Sermon*, 44–47.

11. See Lischer, *Theology of Preaching*, 11, 27.

12. See Buttrick, *Homiletic*, 449–59.

mine. But what I was able to discover confirmed my impression that the theology of preaching is rarely addressed in the contemporary teaching of homiletics in the Episcopal seminaries.

∾

The present situation in regard to preaching and its theological basis has, I believe, roots in the earlier history of Anglicanism. In the early centuries it seemed otherwise, perhaps because of the influence of Lutheranism. The nineteenth Article of Religion, which is derived from Article VII of the Augsburg Confession, states: "The visible Church of Christ is a congregation of faithful men in which the pure Word of God is preached and the sacraments duly administered. . . ." The *Edwardian Book of Homilies*, by Thomas Cranmer and others and published in 1547, contained twelve sermons on the Scriptures, sin, justification, faith, and so forth. The preface states that the purpose of these homilies is to assure that the people are "faithfully instructed in the very [that is, true] word of God" and to assure "the true faith and pure declaring of God's word."[13] Late in the sixteenth century, in his *Laws of Ecclesiastical Polity*, Richard Hooker wrote an extended treatment of the fundamental importance of the reading and preaching of the Word of God in Scripture. He states, "So worthy a part of divine service we should greatly wrong, if we did not esteem Preaching as the blessed ordinance of God, sermons as keys to the kingdom of God, as wings of the soul, unto the sound and healthy as food, as physic unto diseased minds."[14] In the eighteenth century, the foremost Anglican preacher, John Wesley, was also a theologian who held a high doctrine of preaching. In a sermon "Of the Church" he commented on Article 19 in this way: "According to this definition, those congregations in which the 'pure Word of God' (a strong expression) is not preached are no parts of either the Church of England or the Church Catholic," although he was a bit uneasy about the sweeping character of the Article.[15]

---

13. Church of England, *Certain Sermons or Homilies*, 2, 3.

14. Keble, *Works of the Learned*, 1:325a (Bk. 5, chap. 22.1).

15. Outler, *John Wesley*, 313. For any who doubt Wesley's credentials as an Anglican theologian, in 1738 he summarized his doctrinal position over against the Moravians in a condensation of the first five Edwardian Homilies, and in 1790 he stated: "I declare once more that I live and die a member of the Church of England, and none that regard my judgment or advice will ever separate from it." See Wesley, *Works of John Wesley*, 1:10.

In the nineteenth century, however, the situation appears to change. Preaching begins to be subordinated if not ignored. One reason, no doubt, was the Oxford Movement and its revival of Catholic practice. John Henry Newman, a leader of the movement, had this to say in the "Advertisement" to the *Tracts for the Times* about the awakened and anxious sinner who goes to hear dissenting ministers preach: "Had he been taught as a child, that the Sacraments, not preaching, are the sources of divine grace, . . . we would not have so many wanderers from our fold, nor so many cold hearts within it."[16] One indication of how this view spread is the *Theological Introduction to the Thirty-Nine Articles* published in 1919 by E. J. Bicknell. Each of the articles is analyzed in detail, but while Bicknell devotes eighty-four pages to the sacraments there is not one word on preaching, even in his analysis of Article 19. Similarly, in 1935 Paul Elmer More and Frank Leslie Cross published their well-known, eight-hundred-page book, *Anglicanism: The Thought and Practice of the Church of England, Illustrated from the Religious Literature of the Seventeenth Century*. Although over a hundred pages are devoted to the sacraments, not a single page is devoted to preaching. Finally, *Doctrine in the Church of England*, the 1938 report of the Doctrine Commission appointed by the Archbishops of Canterbury and York, although it includes seventy-five pages on the sacraments, has nothing on preaching. I should add that all of these works treat the theology of the sacraments, that is, the relation of God to the sacraments.

It is characteristic of the broadly Catholic tradition that it tends to downplay preaching. In this tradition salvation tends to be interpreted as participation in the divine life or, as in patristic theology, the deification of humanity. The focus is on the Incarnation of Christ as interpreted in the fourth Gospel, and the means of salvation is primarily the sacraments. Accordingly, the theological language is that of being, nature, and substance interpreted by organic and non-personal metaphors. It might be noted in this connection that right down to the Second Vatican Council, preaching was not a constitutive element in the official concept of priesthood in the Roman Catholic Church.[17] In the Protestant tradition, on the other hand, salvation tends to be understood as the restoration of a bro-

16. Newman et al., *Tracts for the Times*, 1:iv.

17. See Council of Trent, Session 23, Canon 1: "If anyone says . . . that those who do not preach are not priests at all: let him be anathema." See Denziger, *Sources of Catholic Dogma*, No. 961.

ken relationship, communion with God through the forgiveness of sin. The focus is on the atonement of Christ in the cross as interpreted in the letters of Paul. The means is primarily the preaching of the Word of God, the word of divine favor and forgiveness. The theological language and metaphors are those of personal relationships. Although Anglicanism claims to combine the Catholic and Protestant traditions and understand them as essential to each other, in recent centuries the tendency has apparently been to emphasize the former in regard to preaching.

∿

Now if my assessment of preaching in the Episcopal Church is at all valid, what is the solution? I suggest that the solution lies in our becoming clear on the theology of preaching, which I have defined as the theology of God's relation to preaching. The initial question is: What can we hope and expect to happen between God and the congregation in and through our preaching? Let us assume that God is always present to all people as creator, sustainer, and potentially as judge and savior. So the question becomes: What, beyond this, is the relation of God to the congregation hearing the sermon? What more can we hope and trust that God is doing specifically in and through the sermon?

A useful way to approach such a theological question is to inquire as to the possible answers.[18] I suggest that there are four possible answers. In and through the sermon, God may be expected:

1. to do nothing unusual;

2. to inspire the hearers to grasp the meaning of the instruction in the sermon;

3. to inspire the hearers to act on the exhortation in the sermon; or

4. to use the sermon to encounter the hearers with a divine word of judgment and mercy.

As suggested above, I believe that the way we answer this question will determine how and what we preach. For example, if we hold the first answer and so have no particular expectations about the relation of God to our preaching, our sermons will be quite different from those

18. See Thomas, *Theological Questions*, appendix and throughout.

we would preach if, for example, our expectation were that God will use "the foolishness of our preaching to save those who believe" (1 Cor 1:21). Now how shall we decide between these answers? Let us follow a common Anglican procedure of assessing them by the criteria of Scripture, tradition, and reason (as the means by which we interpret Scripture and tradition and the contemporary cultural situation).

In regard to Scripture I will not be exhaustive but rather simply indicate relevant passages that need to be interpreted for their theological meaning. Where and how does Scripture address the theology of preaching as defined? The main form of preaching in the Old Testament is that of the prophets. Many passages in the books of the prophets include the words, "The word of the Lord came to the prophet, and he said, 'Thus says the Lord. . . .'" This phrase appears some fifty times in the book of Jeremiah alone. It becomes most explicit in Jer 1:9, "Then the Lord put out his hand and touched my mouth; and the Lord said to me, 'Now I have put my words in your mouth. See today I have appointed you over nations and kingdoms, to pluck up and to pull down, to destroy and to overthrow, to build and to plant." This is explained further in Jer 23:28–29, "Let the prophet who has a dream tell the dream, but let the one who has my word, speak my word faithfully. . . . Is not my word like fire, says the Lord, and like a hammer that breaks a rock in pieces?" The dynamics of this are spelled out in Isa 55:10–11, "For as the rain and snow come down from heaven, and do not return there until they have watered the earth, making it bring forth and sprout, giving seed to the sower and bread to the eater, so shall my word be that goes out of my mouth; it shall not return to me empty, but it shall accomplish that which I purpose, and succeed in the thing for which I sent it."

In the New Testament, preaching is primarily that of Jesus and his followers. Jesus's preaching is essentially the announcement of the good news of presence of the reign of God (Mark 1:14–15) or "speaking the word" to the people (Mark 2:2). "The crowd was pressing in on him to hear the word of God" (Luke 5:1). When a woman cries out that Jesus's mother is blessed, he responds, "Blessed rather are those who hear the word of God and obey it" (Luke 11:28). The same applies to the twelve and the seventy disciples sent out by Jesus to preach and to heal as his representatives. "Whoever listens to you, listens to me, and whoever rejects me rejects the one who sent me" (Luke 10:16). This is explained further in the parable of the sower: "The seed is the word of God" (Luke 8:11).

John's Gospel announces that the word of God, which is God, "became flesh" in Jesus (John 1:14) and proclaims the identity of Jesus as manifest in his works and words with the word of God.

Similarly, the preaching of the apostles after the resurrection is seen as the preaching of the gospel of Christ understood to be the Word of God. In the earliest book in the New Testament, Paul states, "We also constantly give thanks for this, that when you received the word of God that you heard from us, you accepted it not as a human word but as what it really is, God's word, which is at work in you believers" (1 Thess 2:13). Paul understands preaching as involving God's saving approach to the hearers, as in 1 Cor 1:21: "For since, in the wisdom of God, the world did not know God through wisdom, God decided, through the foolishness of our preaching, to save those who believe." The context of this is God's reconciliation of the world through Christ. Paul states, "All this is from God, who reconciled us to himself through Christ, and has given us the ministry of reconciliation; that is, in Christ God was . . . entrusting the message of reconciliation to us. So we are ambassadors for Christ, since God is making his appeal through us; we entreat you on behalf of Christ, be reconciled to God" (2 Cor 5:18–20). Paul stresses the urgency of this in Rom 10:13–14: "But how are they to call on one in whom they have not believed? And how are they to believe in one of whom they have never heard? And how are they to hear without a preacher? . . . So faith comes from what is heard, and what is heard comes through the word of God."

In regard to tradition I interpret the Anglican view to be that, while there is a specifically Anglican tradition, exemplified in the Articles of Religion, Anglican theologians have properly been free to appeal to any part of the orthodox tradition in assessing a theological question.[19] Richard Lischer laments "how few theologies of preaching the Church has produced in the past 1900 years."[20] Although preaching occurred everywhere and always, especially at the Eucharist, apparently the theology of preaching did not become a subject of debate in Christian history until the Reformation. There was much discussion of the theology of the sacraments, beginning in the late fourth century in Augustine's debate with the Donatists, but there was little or no discussion of the theology of preaching before Luther. In Luther, however, the theology of preaching

19. Thomas and Wondra, *Introduction to Theology*, 57–63.
20. Lischer, *Theories of Preaching*, 2.

as the word of God is a constant and powerful theme. The preacher, as he puts it:

> must boldly say with St. Paul and all the apostles and prophets: *Haec dixit dominus*, Thus saith God Himself; or again: In this sermon, I am a confessed apostle and prophet of Jesus Christ. It is neither necessary nor good to ask here for the forgiveness of sins, as though the teaching were false. For it is not my word but God's, which he neither will nor can forgive me, and for which He must always praise and reward me, saving: You have taught rightly for I have spoken through you and the Word is mine. Whoever cannot boast thus of his preaching repudiates preaching; for he expressly denies and slanders God.[21]

Although Calvin's emphasis falls more on the teaching of doctrine as the word of God to the faithful, he understands the importance of the preaching of the word of God in much the same way that Luther did. He speaks of preachers as the "voice" and "mouth" of God, emphasizing the internal testimony of the Spirit. He states, "In the preaching of the Word, the external minister holds forth the vocal word, and it is received by the ears. The internal minister, the Holy Spirit, truly communicates the thing proclaimed through the Word, that is Christ, to the souls of all who will. . . ."[22] I have discussed above the interpretation of the theology of preaching in the Church of England of the sixteenth century. Much of this teaching was repeated in the Protestant orthodox theology of the seventeenth century. During the Pietist and Evangelical movements of the eighteenth century there was a revival of expository preaching, as exemplified in that of Wesley.

Although the liberal theology of the nineteenth century had some of its roots in German pietism, the tendency of this theology was to play down the evangelical style of preaching. The period of liberal theology came to an end in the first quarter of the twentieth century in the work of Karl Barth in which there was a powerful reaffirmation of the theology of preaching of Luther and Calvin. In fact, the whole of his massive thirteen-volume (but unfinished) *Church Dogmatics* is based on the doctrine of the word of God and focuses on the theology of preaching. He begins with a fourteen hundred page prolegomena, entitled "The Doctrine of

21. Weimar Ausgabe 51: 516, 15; quoted in Barth, *Church Dogmatics* I/2, 747.

22. "Summary of Doctrine concerning the Ministry of the Word and Sacraments, VI," in Calvin, *Theological Treatises*, 173.

the Word of God," containing a strong emphasis on preaching or church proclamation as the material of dogmatics. This also contains his theology of preaching, which can be summed up in his explication of the following statement in the Second Helvetic Confession of 1566, the most universal of the Reformed confessions: "The preaching of the Word of God is the Word of God. Wherefore when this Word of God is now preached in the church by preachers lawfully called, we believe that the very Word of God is preached, and received of the faithful."[23] Barth adds, "For a proper explanation of this . . . we should have to refer . . . to the Christological doctrine of the two natures."[24] That is, preaching constitutes an extension of the Incarnation in that it is an action that is fully human and fully divine and mediates a real presence of Christ, as in the Eucharist.

The other theologian who most deeply influenced Christian theology in the twentieth century, and through his students still influences the twenty-first, is Rudolph Bultmann, a colleague of Barth who came later into conflict with him on many issues. Theology in the latter half of the last century was dominated by the issues that divided Barth and Bultmann, but in one respect they are entirely agreed, for Bultmann's emphasis on preaching as the Word of God is even stronger than Barth's. Bultmann, interpreting Paul, states, "The salvation occurrence is nowhere present except in the proclaiming, accosting, demanding, and promising word of preaching."[25] And in the context of the demythologizing debate, he writes, "Christ meets us in the preaching as one crucified and risen. He meets us in the word of preaching and nowhere else. . . . The word of preaching confronts us as the word of God. It is not for us to question its credentials. It is we who are questioned, we who are asked whether we will believe the word or reject it."[26]

Here we may conclude this brief summary of some of the main points in the Christian tradition on the theology of preaching.[27] There is little to add from the last fifty years. Important theological movements have, of course, taken place—liberation theology in its various forms (feminist, black, Latin American, and so forth), ecological theology, and

23. See Leith, *Creeds of the Churches*, 133.

24. Barth, *Church Dogmatics* I/I, 2nd ed., 52.

25. Bultmann, *Theology of the New Testament*, 1:302.

26. Bultmann, *Kerygma and Myth: A Theological Debate*, 41.

27. For a survey of the theology of preaching from the New Testament to the modern period, consult Cooke, *Ministry to Word and Sacraments*, pt. 2.

various theologies from Asia and Africa. As far as I know, however, none of these has emphasized the theology of preaching.

In summary I suggest that the majority of the testimony of Scripture and tradition interpreted by reason supports the fourth answer to our question. What can we hope and expect will happen between God and the congregation in and through our preaching? We can hope that God will use the sermon to encounter the hearers with a divine word of judgment and mercy. (Here I might add that the theology of preaching implied in the service for the ordination of a priest in the *Book of Common Prayer* is consistent with this answer.[28]) The argument I have given has been only an outline. It may be that other arguments could be made that would lead to different conclusions. I would nevertheless maintain that my argument and its conclusion are valid possibilities, and I would note that they are confirmed by the fact that the position I have taken is practically identical with the theology of preaching of a leading Anglican theologian, John Macquarrie,[29] and with that of two of the leading contemporary homileticians, David Buttrick and William Willimon.[30]

∾

Now what does the foregoing argument have to say about what must be involved in preaching? If Scripture is understood in the tradition as the Word of God, that is, as testimony to the revelation of God in the history of Israel culminating in Christ, then preaching, understood also as the Word God, must be the reiteration of the prophetic and apostolic testimony in Scripture. That is the chief point. It does not mean that preaching is a mechanical repetition of Scripture but rather that it is a creative interpretation and application, to the situation of the hearers, of the scriptural testimony.

A second point follows. There are not several types of sermons, for example, expository, historical, doctrinal, moral, apologetic, and topical. There is only one, namely expository preaching. The promise of Scripture and tradition that "the one who hears you hears me," that the words of the

28. See the 1979 *Book of Common Prayer*, 526, 532, 534.

29. See Macquarrie, *Principles of Christian Theology*, 387–88, 397–98, 400, 403–4, 405–6.

30. See Buttrick, *Homiletic*, 449–59; and Willimon, *Pastor*, 141–70, which is a summary of his two earlier books on homiletics.

preacher can be used by God to encounter the hearers in judgment and mercy, is based on preaching being expository, the attempt to interpret and apply a passage of Scripture to the situation of the hearers.[31]

From these basic points, some practical consequences can be drawn. The preparation of a sermon begins with the selection of a passage of Scripture from the Gospel, epistle, or Old Testament readings for the day. It begins, in other words, with a passage from one among assigned texts, not from a passage freely chosen by us that makes some point we want to preach about. Furthermore, the text should be a passage of more than one or two verses, because the shorter the text, the greater the temptation to use it as a pretext for our own ideas rather than those of the text. Then should come prayer that the Spirit will open and illumine our minds to understand the meaning of the testimony of this passage to God in Christ. This will involve our willingness to subordinate provisionally all our ideas, images, and convictions to the text in order to hear its testimony without distortion.

The work of actually producing the sermon requires three steps: exegesis, translation, and application.

1. The first step, exegesis, is the attempt to determine the intention and meaning of the passage in its historical context, situation, and terms. Here we are greatly assisted by the literary and historical-critical study of the Bible over the past century issuing in a range of dictionaries, general commentaries, studies of individual books, and other reference works. With what these are, and how to use them, the sermon-writer ought to be thoroughly acquainted. We may not be professional exegetes, but we can become familiar enough with their methods and procedures so that we can do some of it ourselves and check their conclusions.

2. The next step is meditation on this meaning, to allow it to speak to us, and then its translation into the language, the concepts, and the metaphors of our own day. (I am aware of the criticism of the use of the metaphor of translation here, and I have responded to it in *Theological Questions*, 16–18.) This is already begun in the first step in the process of understanding the intention and meaning

---

31. For a fuller elaboration of this argument, see Van Buren, "Word of God in the Church."

of the original text. And it already involves the beginning of the third step.

3. The final step is the application of this intention and meaning to the situation of the hearers. This is a demanding process that involves creativity and imagination on the part of the preacher. It requires an understanding of the general cultural situation of the modern world, where it came from and where it is going, and also the special version of this, which obtains in the congregation of hearers with their own particular issues. This requires a continuing discipline of reading from the daily newspaper, interpretive journals, and broader studies.[32]

This summary of the process of expository preaching oversimplifies an extremely complex process that has been analyzed over the past two centuries in the discipline of hermeneutics.[33] Krister Stendahl has encapsulated it in the metaphor of the bilingual translator who knows the languages of the biblical world and of the modern world and can move around in each with idiomatic ease and thus relate them at particular points. He concludes, "The task of the pulpit is—as suggested here the true *Sitz im Leben*, 'life situation,' where the meaning of the original meets with the meaning for today."[34]

Nothing in what I have proposed is meant to deny what Article 19 plainly affirms, namely an equality of word and sacrament as marks of the "visible church of Christ," for the word leads to the sacrament and is fulfilled in the sacrament. Without the word the sacrament tends to become a strange mystery, which is easily misunderstood. Without the sacrament the Word is unfulfilled, not acted out. Macquarrie speaks of the unity, mutual necessity, inseparability, and importance of a "proper balance" between the word and the sacraments.[35] In Anglicanism we are strong on the sacraments. It is perhaps our greatest strength. But we have been weak on the word. A sign of this to me is that while we begin and end the

32. Two examples of the sort of study I have in mind are Bellah et al., *Habits of the Heart*, and Putnam, *Bowling Alone*.

33. For an introduction to this discipline, see Thiselton, *Two Horizons*.

34. Stendahl, "Biblical Theology," 1:430–31. Stendahl's essay has produced a major debate. For a summary of this and a constructive revision, see Wilson, "Biblical Studies and Preaching: A Growing Divide?" in Long and Farley, *Preaching as a Theological Task*.

35. Macquarrie, *Principles of Christian Theology*, 387, 399, 421.

Eucharist with many prayers, we tend to begin and end the sermon with none. And my point is that our weakness in regard to the word tends to have a deleterious effect on the sacraments in our common life.

Furthermore, I believe that this approach to preaching will solve some of the problems faced by the preacher. Taken together with the liturgical lectionary, it will solve the problem of what to preach about, although the choice of a specific text remains. Also it will help to solve one of the problems of the beginning preacher—a problem, which persists for even the most experienced one—namely, anxiety about preaching. I believe that this anxiety derives in large part from a concern to do well, a worry about what people will think of the sermon, and a desire to be admired as a preacher. This problem is only aggravated if the sermon consists mainly of the preacher's own experience or the ideas or views he or she happens to have about some topic or other. In expository preaching this problem is avoided in large part because attention is taken off the preacher, the preacher's ideas, personality, manner, delivery, and performance, and transferred to the text, where it belongs.

I believe that the theology of preaching that I have outlined, and the necessity of expository preaching to which it leads, present an exciting challenge and opportunity. It is an awesome and solemn thought that God may use our preaching as the divine approach to the hearers, as the means of his saving presence to them, that God may use the "foolishness" of our preaching to save those who believe. Furthermore, I believe that many people attend church today hungering for the gospel. I will never forget one evening at a closed Al-Anon meeting, which was subverted by a couple of visitors who were obviously not living with an alcoholic. After a while an older woman in the back row stood up and said quietly, "Look, I came here tonight because I decided not to commit suicide . . . yet. These meetings are a matter of life and death for me, and you are ruining them. So please shut up or leave." My point is that the preacher never knows, but should always assume, that there are going to be some people in church every Sunday—and perhaps the same applies to everyone present, in some degree—for whom this service, this Eucharist, this sermon, may be a matter of life and death. We who preach should never fail to preach the gospel.

CHAPTER SEVEN

Prayer in Anglican Practice

THE BASIS OF PRAYER in Anglican practice is, of course, *The Book of Common Prayer*. Wakefield describes it as:

> a book for the laity, for the whole people of God in their daily lives. It is the foundation of family religion, of domestic piety. This is why the offices, by Cranmer's sheer genius, are reduced [from eight] to two—morning and evening prayer—to be said daily throughout the year, so that ordinary men and women may begin and end the day with devotions that will not depend on moods or circumstances but will enable them to join with the great church in hearing the word of God and offering most worthy praise.[1]

The *Prayer Book*, however, has always been supplemented by books of prayers for various occasions beginning with *The Primer of 1559* and Matthew Wren's *A Collection of Private Devotions* (1626) down to such works as Carl G. Carlozzi's *Prayers for Pastor and People* (1984).

The collects of the *Prayer Book* have been drawn from many sources and have been refined over many centuries as expressions of Christian faith, hope, and love. They have proven to be useful and important to a wide range of people in giving voice to their deepest concerns in a variety of circumstances. A constant danger in set forms of prayer, however, is over-familiarity that can lead to boredom and a sense of irrelevance. This, in turn, can lead to a fundamental mistake in prayer, namely, dishonesty or the failure to begin where we are.

1. Wakefield, "Anglican Spirituality," 261.

I believe that this is the main reason that prayer often seems so bor-ing and irrelevant and the requirement of prayer so guilt-producing for many today. We hear or read learned treatises on prayer and the various stages of prayer. We hear that prayer should begin with adoration and praise, move on to penitence and confession, then thanksgiving, finally to intercession and petition, concluding with contemplation. So when we begin to pray and try to put all this into practice, it often feels lifeless and dull. The reason for this, I believe, is that we have aimed too high. We have tried to begin where we believe the saints are. We have not begun where *we* are. This, I believe, is the first and most common mistake in prayer. And the way to correct this mistake is simply to begin where we are. How does one do this? What do you think about when your mind wanders from what you are doing? What do you think of when you wake up in the middle of the night? What worries or troubles you right now? Or on the other hand, what is it that makes you happy right now? That is where you are in the present, and that is where you should begin your prayer.

The reason that we must begin our prayers this way is that this is who we really are. God does not want what we believe to be perfect prayer, our piety and devotion. God wants us as we really are with all our doubts, fears, anxieties, joys, longings, and bitternesses. If, however, we are dishonest in our prayer and attempt to be something that we are not, if we hide ourselves behind our dishonest prayer, God will not be able to get at us through our prayer, but will have to get at us in some other way, perhaps through tragedy.

Now it may be a great relief to hear that God wants us just as we are (see Hymn 693), that God really wants us to be honest. But it may sound incredible, for the Christian gospel has always sounded incredible. The good news of the gospel is that God in Christ meets us where we are and accepts us as we are, that God has come to us when we could not go to God, that we are right with God through God's gift in Christ, that we are justified by faith, by trust in God's grace in Christ. Therefore, we can come before God as we are, because God sees us as righteous in Christ. That is why even as beginners in prayer we can offer our simple, real, honest prayers to God through Christ, because God in Christ has opened up a new way for us to come in the presence of God as we are.

If this sounds as though Christian prayer is being watered down, then 2 Cor 12 should be consulted in which Paul describes his growth in prayer. He has a thorn in the flesh, some embarrassing affliction that hinders him in his preaching. He is honest before God and fervently asks God to take away this affliction, not once but three times. God, however, says No, "My grace is sufficient for you, for my power is made perfect in weakness." And Paul's prayer becomes one of thanksgiving: "I will all the more gladly boast of my weaknesses, that the power of Christ may rest upon me."

The Bible is full of great prayer, because it is full of honest prayer, real wrestling with God. The people of God bear the name Israel, which probably means the one who "wrestles God." Job and the Psalmist wrestled with God. They did not like the way God was running things. So they went into the presence of God with honest anger, bitterness, and despair and they cried out to God. They wrestled with God, and God pinned them and transformed them and they came to trust and praise God.

Jesus taught his followers to wrestle with God in prayer. When they asked him to teach them how to pray, he told them that strange parable about the importunate friend who came to his neighbor at midnight, beat on the door and routed him out of bed to lend some bread for a late arriving guest. Jesus says that he will not get up and help him because he is his friend, but because of his importunity, his troublesome persistence. And the point of the parable is, "Ask, and it will be given you, seek, and you will find; knock, and it will be opened to you" (Luke 11:9). Later, he also told them the parable of the unjust judge "to the effect that they ought always to pray and not lose heart" (Luke 18:1). There was a judge who was no respecter of persons, and there was a widow who kept coming to him and demanding that he vindicate her against her adversary. Although the judge did not play favorites, he finally grants her request, not because of the righteousness of her cause but in order to be rid of her complaining. Jesus concludes, "And will not God vindicate his elect who cry to him day and night?" (Luke 18:7)

And Jesus practiced what he taught. In the Garden of Gethsemane he wrestled with God to the end. "Father, if you are willing, remove this cup from me. . . . And being in agony he prayed more earnestly; and his sweat became like great drops of blood falling down upon the ground" (Luke 22:42, 44). And to Jesus's most urgent and honest prayer God said No. So Jesus suffered death and passed through it to resurrection and new life. This is the path that Christians are called to follow as wrestlers with God who are honest in prayer.

Anglican theologian John Burnaby summarizes all this as follows:

> The first rule of prayer is sincerity. Our desires and our needs are the most vital part of us; and God's children may not approach their Father with a feigned devotion, fearing to tell him what we really want. If I am to learn what God wants, the way to do it is not to disown the inmost desires of my heart, but rather deliberately to spread them out before God—to face with all the honesty I can achieve the real truth about my desires, to wrestle with the sham of professing desires which are not really mine, and *then* to pray. Then, no doubt, I shall find that there are things, desirable in themselves, which the Christian who prays in charity cannot ask God to give him, because neither love of God nor love of neighbor would be served by their possession. For prayer itself will be the schooling of desire.[2]

Burnaby supports this interpretation of prayer by exploring how the earliest Christians prayed as indicated in the New Testament. Offering many examples, he states, "Prayer in the New Testament means quite simply that part of our communion with God which consists in *petition*." Furthermore, "Every clause in the Lord's Prayer is petition." Finally, "Of the prayers of Christ himself . . . in the little that the Gospels have to tell us, petition and intercession, with thanksgiving, make up the whole."[3] Burnaby concludes,

> Petition is present everywhere in the most important part of the Church's liturgical inheritance from Judaism—the Psalms; and petitionary prayer has continued to be the dominating element in Christian worship, both Catholic and Reformed: witness the long series of Collects for Sundays and Holy Days in the Book of Common Prayer.[4]

Burnaby notes, however, that the majority of the Christian tradition on prayer is opposed to this emphasis on petition. He states,

> Yet within the Christian Church a great tradition of mystical theology has thrived on the genius and the teachings of some of the noblest examples of Catholic sainthood. The vast literature of Christian prayer has been predominantly occupied with the

2. John Burnaby, "Christian Prayer," in Vidler, *Soundings*, 234–35.
3. Ibid., 223.
4. Ibid., 224.

technique of contemplation and the 'practice of the presence of God' to which the saints have shown the way. The consequence of this preoccupation has been to suggest that the use of vocal prayer is no more than an elementary stage in the Christian life, and in particular that petition is an act or attitude which *ought* to be superseded, as we come to know better what it means to lift up our hearts to God. If this is true, our inherited forms of Common Prayer, which are both vocal and to a large extent petitionary, will not serve to train us in these higher reaches of communion with God. We shall either acquiesce in the existence of a double standard in the life of prayer—one for the expert and one for the ordinary believer—or we shall be tempted to abandon the practice of both public and private prayer as we have known it, and take the easy way of reducing our devotions to a vague and planless meditation.[5]

This majority of the Christian tradition, which has been occupied with contemplation, has been greatly strengthened in the last four decades by the new Romantic movement and its offshoot in the spirituality movement.[6] The foundation of these movements has been largely in the perennial philosophy and in particular Neoplatonism.[7] This has resulted in the emphasis in the current spirituality movement on the interior life, the mystical, the apophatic, and deification or theosis, all achieved through contemplative prayer. The revival of interest in contemplative prayer has been led by the centering prayer movement and especially by Fr. Thomas Keating, a Cistercian monk. He states,

> During the first sixteen centuries of Church history, contemplative prayer was the acknowledged goal of Christian spirituality. After the Reformation, this heritage, at least as a living tradition, was virtually lost. Now in the twentieth century . . . the recovery of the Christian contemplative tradition has begun. The method of centering prayer . . . is contributing to this renewal.[8]

5. Ibid., 222.

6. See chapter 3.

7. See my essay, "Christianity and the Perennial Philosophy," in *What Is It That Theologians Do*, ch. 12.

8. Keating, *Open Mind, Open Heart*, 143. See also Pennington, *Centering Prayer*; and D. Taylor, *Becoming Christ*.

He defines contemplative prayer as "a process of interior transformation, a conversation initiated by God and leading, if we consent, to divine union." "Divine union is the goal of all Christians."[9] He states, "I prefer to use the terms *contemplation* and *mysticism* to mean the same thing." "The essence of mysticism is the path of pure faith." Keating seems to identify "pure faith," "the experience of emptiness," "pure consciousness," and "union with God." According to Keating, centering prayer can lead to "pure consciousness." "In that state there is no awareness of self. . . . This is what divine union is."[10]

As in the case of the attitude toward Platonism, so here also there is always the possibility for a synthesis. An example of such a synthesis can be found in the writing of William Temple, Archbishop of Canterbury in the 1940s. He states, on the one hand, that "the aim of all prayer is the same as the aim of all life, it is union with God." On the other hand, he also affirms that petitionary prayer is the essential form of prayer. Why?

> Because there may be blessings which are only effectively bless-
> ings to those who are in the right condition of mind. . . . The way
> to recognize that [God] is the source of the blessings, and we need
> them, is to ask. . . . In our Lord's teaching about petitionary prayer
> there are three main principles. The first is confidence, the second
> is perseverance, and the third . . . correspondence . . . [namely]
> prayer offered in [Christ's] name.[11]

The proponents of centering prayer and contemplation suggest that their practice should require about thirty to forty-five minutes per day. This is more than the time required for the daily office of Morning or Evening Prayer and is apparently a substitute for it. This, however, does not fit with Anglican practice as Burnaby and I have interpreted it.

---

9. Ibid., 4, 33.

10. Ibid., 10–11, 73–74.

11. Temple, *Christian Faith and Life*, 106–8, 111–13.

CHAPTER EIGHT

The Story of Two Communities

FOR A LONG TIME I have noted, both in my own work and that of others, that theology is usually done backwards. By this I mean that convictions in theology and moral theology are usually arrived at by deep and complex processes nurtured by experience and intuition, processes of which we are largely unaware, rather than by conscious rational reflection. Then these convictions are articulated and tested by means of theological reflection on scripture and tradition. Needless to say, this reflection in turn influences experience and intuition.

I can put this another way by noting the importance of the sociology of theology. That is, the social-cultural context (race, class, sex) in which theology is carried out is highly influential in the development of theological and moral convictions. I recall that colleagues and students whom I had come to know at the Episcopal Divinity School and who moved to quite different contexts developed rather different theological and moral convictions. For example, I remember one of the best students I ever had, who was a conservative Anglo-Catholic in theology but who after teaching many years in the philosophy and religion department of a large midwestern state university gradually became an agnostic Unitarian Universalist. He agrees that his context has been very influential in the development of his convictions.

I am not proposing the extreme position taken by some sociologists of knowledge, which holds that rational reflection is merely an epiphenomenon or by-product of psycho-socio-cultural factors, but only that these factors are always influential and sometimes highly influential in the development of theological and moral convictions. They are not, however, determinative; otherwise, why spend your life studying and teaching theology?

Now in regard to the current debate in the Episcopal Church about sexuality and especially homosexuality, I have the impression from reading many of the books and essays that have been produced in the course of this struggle that most of the exegetical, historical, theological, moral, and pastoral issues have been discussed quite thoroughly. And I hazard the guess that nothing radically new and decisive can be expected from this quarter. (I hope I am entirely open to being persuaded otherwise.) Therefore I suggest that we need to discuss the so-called non-theological factors in the debate.

The Episcopal Church is comprised of a large number of very diverse communities of worship and discourse with long traditions of diverse experience and intuition. I suspect that our divisions over issues in sexuality are derived in large part from this diversity. Therefore, I propose that one way forward in the discussion is to address ourselves to this diversity of communal experience in order better to understand how we have come to differ and to learn from each other's experience and intuition. Here I want to recount the stories of the ways in which two communities of faith of which I have been a member have dealt with issues having to do with homosexuality. One is the Episcopal Theological (now Divinity) School, of which I have been a member as student and teacher for forty-four years, and the other is the Church of St. John the Evangelist on Bowdoin Street in Boston, of which I have been a member for seventeen years.

The Episcopal Theological School was founded in 1867 by a group of laymen who agreed that it should have a lay board of trustees in order to avoid ecclesiastical interference, and that it should be near to and affiliated with Harvard University in order to offer the best academic instruction. In 1974 the school merged with the Philadelphia Divinity School, which had a similar background. Off and on throughout its history, the school has been in trouble with various parts of the Episcopal Church—for example, for introducing the historical-critical approach to the Bible, for harboring a radical ethicist who was the founder of modern medical ethics and situation ethics, for admitting women for the MDiv degree, for advocating the ordination of women, for employing two women whose ordinations were at the time deemed irregular (though they were regularized within the year), and for admitting openly homosexual students. For these reasons, there has been tension between the school and some other parts of the church. The school has always believed that it was the right kind of tension, however, because it derived from an attempt to deal with issues that were facing the church. It is primarily this last issue of homosexuality that is dividing the church at present. It is well known that the church has ordained homosexual men from the beginning. (And if the late Yale historian John Boswell is correct, the church has blessed homosexual unions from the early centuries.) The same applies to the Episcopal Church. Probably all Episcopal seminaries have admitted and graduated homosexual people who have then been ordained in virtually all the dioceses of the church. Probably most of them have been sexually active. In the past when the issue of homosexuality came into the open, usually through some complaint or scandal, it was handled secretly. When one of my seminary classmates disappeared overnight with no explanation, it was rumored that he had been involved in some homosexual "incident," and I have heard of similar occurrences in other Episcopal seminaries. Secrecy was the name of the game. What is new in the last quarter of this century is the appearance at seminary doors of openly gay and lesbian people, often in committed relationships, and also the beginning of the end of secrecy.

About twenty-five years ago an openly gay man applied for admission to the Episcopal Theological School. His application was discussed in the admissions committee, of which I was a member, and it was decided that the question of his admission required broader consideration among the various constituencies of the school. Over a period of months consultations were held among faculty, trustees, students, graduates, and benefactors, along with some outside consultants, namely, psychiatrists and psychologists. Finally a unanimous decision was made by the faculty trustees, and the school senate of faculty, students, and staff not to discriminate against people because of their sexual orientation. This included offering seminary housing for gay and lesbian couples. The same decision was made later in regard to faculty.

Over the years since then, a number of openly gay and lesbian people have been admitted, graduated, and ordained in several dioceses.

The percentage of gay and lesbian members of the school has probably been somewhat higher in recent years than in society at large, because it is considered to be a relatively safe place for them to live openly. While there are presumably considerable numbers of gay and lesbian students at all the other Episcopal seminaries, their degree of openness varies with the policy of the seminary.

Over the past quarter century we straights and gays at EDS have come to know, appreciate, admire, and love one another, and work together in this particular area of the church's life and ministry. For example, I recall a long discussion in a small conference group of first-year students with a young gay man about his homosexuality—when he realized it, whether any choice was involved, what it was like to live in a largely homophobic society. I also remember another discussion in a conference group of second-year students with a young lesbian woman who "came out" to us and wanted to talk about coming out to her parents during the Christmas vacation that was approaching. (She is now the rector of a large urban parish.) Finally, I recall after chapel one morning a colleague coming out to me and explaining that he had informed his bishop before he was ordained in the 1950s. This is the kind of experience of trust, friendship, and interchange that has brought the school community and myself to where we are today, and it has enriched our lives greatly. We believe that we are modeling a kind of inclusive community life for the church at large. This is not to say that there have not been tensions, cliquishness, backbiting, and so forth. Before coming to the school, many straight students have never known any gay or lesbian people, especially any who were open about their sexual orientation and feeling confident in being part of a critical mass. Their reactions were similar to those of many men when the number of women students came to equal and then surpass theirs in the 1980s.

It is the policy of EDS to gather a community of diverse people who reflect society at large and to challenge them to deal with real differences and otherness. The suspicion, fear, and hatred of those who are different is the fundamental disease tearing the world apart today, whether in Bosnia, the Middle East, Rwanda, or the inner cities of our nation. In relation to this issue, however, the model of community that the church has adopted in the past half century is a disastrous one for church and society. Based on interpersonal transparency and intimacy, and exalting feelings of belongingness, it is disastrous because it requires homogeneity and the exclusion of those who are different.[1] So the school is seeking a new model of community that rejoices in difference, including difference in sexual orientation. The search is difficult but greatly rewarding.

∾

In 1979 my wife and I began attending regularly the Mission Church of St. John the Evangelist on Bowdoin Street. Located on the "wrong" side of Beacon Hill in Boston, it is one of the great old Anglo-Catholic parishes on the eastern seaboard. The church was built in 1831 as a Congregational church under the leadership of my great-great-uncle, the Rev. Lyman Beecher, father of a wild clan that included the abolitionist preacher Henry Ward Beecher and the author Harriet Beecher Stowe. In 1870 the building was purchased by the Episcopal Church of the Advent, and the Society of St. John the Evangelist, the oldest Anglican men's religious order, was asked to supply the ordained ministry.

In 1882 the Church of the Advent moved to a new building on Brimmer Street, on the "right" side of Beacon Hill, and the Society, commonly known as the "Cowley Fathers" from their original house near Oxford, took over the building on Bowdoin Street as its mission church to the down-and-out, homeless, drunks, pimps, and prostitutes of nearby Scollay Square. The brothers of SSJE lived in the Mission House next door until 1939, when all but four or five moved to their new monastery on Memorial Drive in Cambridge. In the 1960s Scollay Square was replaced by the new Government Center, but the northeast side of Beacon Hill remained an area of cheap rooming houses for the destitute and the aged as well as an area where the homeless gathered. During the first half of this century St. John's was also renowned for its elaborate Anglo-Catholic liturgy and its fine liturgical music under the direction of Everett Titcomb.

In 1976, in reaction to the vote of the General Convention to ordain women to the priesthood and the episcopate, the vicar of St. John's, who was a member of SSJE, and his assistant announced that they were resigning and walked out in the middle of the eucharist. Both became Roman Catholics. After that St. John's was served by vicars of SSJE who were not brothers, and in the late 1970s the parish sponsored for ordination one of the first women priests in the diocese. In 1985 St. John's became an

---

1. See Iris Marion Young, "The Ideal of Community and the Politics of Difference," in Nicholson, *Feminism/Postmodernism.*

independent parish of the diocese, while maintaining a close and friendly relation with SSJE. It has also continued to be an important center for ministry to the homeless, the needy, and shut-ins in the area through programs such as its Jubilee Senior Action Center, Neighborhood Action, Doorbell Ministry, and Food Pantry, as well as a diocesan center for instruction in liturgy and liturgical music.

For the past century St. John's has also been known as a parish where gay and lesbian people are welcome, and many of them have been regular members of the parish and parish officials. At the turn of the century, two distinguished church architects, Ralph Adams Cram, who designed the reredos and collaborated on the stained glass, and Henry Vaughan, who designed the rood screen, were members.[2] Today the Boston chapter of Dignity, the organization of gay and lesbian Roman Catholics, holds its meetings and services at St. John's. It has long been a part of parish lore at St. John's that for many years the clergy have quietly given blessings to same-sex couples. It would be difficult to pin down the facts about this, but the very existence of this oral tradition indicates the attitude of the parish. As at EDS, the presence of relatively large numbers of openly gay and lesbian parishioners has caused tensions and arguments, and some parishioners, both gay and straight, have left. There have been similar reactions to the presence of street people. But as at the school, the goal has been to create a community that accepts and rejoices in real difference and diversity.

The 1980s were marked by both joy and sadness at St. John's. One of the high points in the life of the parish was the annual Wardens' Ball just before Lent. Gay and straight couples and individuals in formal dress or costume came to party, eat, drink, and dance. Straight men and women danced with gay men and lesbian women amidst general rejoicing. The binary was totally problematized, as they say in feminist theory.

The source of sadness was that some members of St. John's had contracted AIDS and were dying. The feeling in the parish was that while there was a lot of mourning focused on the gay membership of the parish, there was also a lot to celebrate in their lives with us. Why was it that we seemed only to bury our gay members and not bless their unions? In 1989 the co-rectors, the Revs. Jennifer Phillips and the Reverend Richard

2. For details see Douglas Shand-Tucci, *Boston Bohemia 1881–1900*, vol. 1 of Shand-Tucci, *Ralph Adams Cram*.

Valantasis, informed Bishop David Johnson that, at the request of some gay and lesbian couples at St. John's, they were going to begin blessing committed same-sex relationships, which they understood as falling under their pastoral prerogative and responsibility. In response Bishop Johnson issued a formal inhibition forbidding them to proceed with the blessings. The parish, upset by this, invited the three bishops of the diocese to St. John's for an evening of discussion.

So in the fall of 1989 Bishop Johnson, Suffragan Bishop Barbara Harris, and Assistant Bishop David Birney all came to St. John's for one of the most remarkable evenings I have ever experienced in the church. Lisa Gary, the senior warden, presided and members of the parish were invited to address themselves not only to the issue of same-sex blessings but also to what it meant to them to live and worship in a congregation that included many openly gay and lesbian individuals and couples. For two hours, individuals and couples, gay and straight, stood up and spoke with great eloquence about how much it meant to them to work, worship, and celebrate at St. John's. There were many expressions of deep Christian piety and heartfelt gratitude for St. John's because of its inclusiveness and openness, especially to gay and lesbian people but also to homeless and street people. The clergy did not speak, but at the end each of the bishops did, saying they had been moved and assuring the congregation that they had been heard.

Discussions between the co-rectors and Bishop Johnson continued, and finally he agreed that St. John's could go ahead with the blessing of same-sex couples, so long as the blessings did not take place in the context of the eucharist. (They were in fact conducted just before the Eucharist.) A process of exploration, instruction, and discussion about blessings, same-sex covenants, and marriage had been going on for some time in the parish. The results of this process have been summarized in this description of parish policy by the Reverend Jennifer Phillips:

> Every household of the community—whether a person living alone, a couple, a person or persons raising children or caring for aging parents, groups of friends, or those making their home temporarily or permanently within a large institution—is called to order itself as a small church community in which God is made manifest, hospitality offered and baptismal vows lived out. Over time, the wider community in its relationship with a household can discern whether that household shows forth God and builds

up the community or not. . . . Where a household is discerned to be filled with love, respect, kindness and prayer, where it reaches out in care to others, where wrongs are forgiven and labor shared, the community rightly desires to return thanks to God for it. And when a couple find in one another a source of joy and comfort, strength in adversity, the knowledge and love of God, then they properly desire to return thanks to God for their relationship and to ask God's continued blessing and the community's prayerful support.[3]

The first blessing, in the fall of 1990, was of two former Roman Catholic nuns who had been committed to each other for seventeen years. I was privileged to assist the rectors at this blessing. It was a time of some anxiety and fear, but also of great rejoicing at St. John's. Because of increased violence against gay and lesbian people in the Boston area as well as other parts of the country, there was serious concern that some person or group might try to interrupt the service or attack the couple. When in the middle of the service someone dropped a book in the back of the church, everyone jumped. Later, after having dinner at this couple's house, my wife happened to mention it to her daughter, who asked with some surprise, "Where do you ever meet lesbians?" My wife responded, "Oh, at church." The following year my wife and I served as sponsors at the blessing of another lesbian couple, and the next summer we served as sponsors for a straight couple.

One of the most recent blessings took place in August 1994, when the union of a theology professor at Boston College and his partner of many years was blessed at St. John's. (The professor is a lay associate of SSJE and for several years he and his partner have conducted retreats for gay couples sponsored by the Society.) Many of the brothers of SSJE attended the blessing, including the present Superior and his predecessor, who is now Bishop of Massachusetts. A large and joyous reception for the couple and the whole parish was held after the service at Emery House, the Society's retreat center in West Newbury, Massachusetts.

This has been the story of how two communities of faith of which I have been privileged to be a member have dealt with the issue of homosexual-

3. Phillips, "Same-Sex Unions," 28.

ity in the church. At the school we made a decision of faith on a complex and difficult issue, and as a result enriched our life with the presence of openly gay and lesbian people. At the parish we came to be aware of a deep pastoral need, worked with the bishop to find a way to meet this need, and as a result brought gay and lesbian people into a fuller participation in our life together as parish. I hardly need to say that this experience has been a very important factor in my present conviction that homosexual people should not be discriminated against in the church in any way, especially in regard to ordination or blessing. If those who differ with me on this issue had had the same experience as I have had in these two communities, I believe that they would be at least nearer to my view than they are now

At the beginning I suggested that convictions in theology and moral theology arrived at by the processes of experience and intuition should be articulated and tested by means of theological reflection on scripture and tradition. This is what we as a church have been doing over the past decade in the large number of discussions, conferences, books, and articles on issues concerning homosexuality. I have been a participant in this process. My judgment, as I have said, is that the exegetical, historical, theological, and moral issues have been discussed thoroughly, and that sufficient grounds have been found for going either way on the issue of the ordination (and blessing) of homosexuals in committed relationships, although it is my conviction that the grounds are stronger for a policy of nondiscrimination. My experience, confirmed by theological reflection, has led me to the conviction that it is time for the Episcopal Church to affirm and regularize what is already happening in this regard.

Since I am aware that the experience of others, confirmed by their own theological reflection, has led them to the opposite conviction, I must add one point. When I refer to experience here, I firmly believe that Christian love and justice require that this experience include firsthand knowledge of and friendship with more than one or two gay or lesbian people and couples. The alternative is to rely on stereotypes, hearsay, gossip, and so forth. The reason for stressing this point is that we live in one of the most homophobic societies in the non-Islamic world, a society in which discrimination and violence against homosexual people is increasing, a society which is moving steadily in a politically and religiously conservative direction, and a society in which anti-homosexual feelings, beliefs, laws, and actions are on the increase. In such a society any "experience" of gay and lesbian people that is not informed by a wider personal knowledge and friendship is liable to be very negative.

My experience, then, including that of the two communities in which I have lived, has been decisive on these issues. Now those who are acquainted with my writing on the relation of experience and theology may wonder at this conclusion, since there I have argued that experience cannot be the main criterion in theological judgment. On the issues under discussion, however, my experience has not been the main criterion but rather a supplementary one. I put it this way in 1983:

> Christian religious experience can be used as a criterion in theology subordinate to scripture and tradition. It can function to confirm or question theological proposals grounded on these authorities. A common situation in theology is that of judging between alternative proposals. When the appeal to scripture and tradition is equally well grounded for two proposals, then that proposal is to be favored which is more complementary with Christian experience, that is, which orders, makes sense of, gives meaning to, and thus interprets the experience more successfully than the other.[4]

This is a version of the position taken by my teacher Paul Tillich. He argues against the appeal to experience in theology and concludes that experience is the medium through which the norms of scripture and tradition speak to us, but that experience itself is not the norm. According to Tillich, the productive power of experience is limited to the transformation of what is given to it. This should be neither simply a repetition of the tradition nor an entirely new production. Thus our experience affects how we understand and interpret scripture and tradition.[5] I see this as an accurate description of how I have come to my views on the issues confronting the church.

Some years ago the dean of the Episcopal Divinity School was challenged by a Greek Orthodox priest who claimed that after befriending the Orthodox in America, the Episcopal Church had betrayed them by ordaining women. The dean replied, "That reminds me of the Episcopalian who was asked if he believed in infant baptism. He responded, 'Believe it?

---

4. From Thomas, "Should experience be the main criterion of theology?" chapter 3 of Thomas, *Theological Questions*, 32. For a more extensive treatment see my essay "Theology and Experience," *What Is It That Theologians Do*, chapter 2.

5. See Tillich, *Systematic Theology*, vol. 1, 40–46.

I've seen it!' So, as regards the ordination of women, I can say, 'We have seen it, and we wish you could too." And so also, in regard to the ordination and blessing of gay and lesbian people, I can say, "We have seen it, and we want you to see it too."

APPENDIX: HYSTERIA OVER HOMOSEXUALITY

WHY IS THE UNITED States probably the only non-Muslim nation in the world that is having hysteria ("excessive anxiety," *Webster's New World Dictionary*) over sexuality in general and homosexuality in particular? For example, the U. S. is the only such nation in which a national chief executive could be impeached for allegedly lying about a consensual act of oral sex, a situation that I believe to be unimaginable in any western European nation. And why is it that American churches are the only churches in this world having such a severe case of hysteria over homosexuality? For example, the Episcopal Church is probably the only church in this world in which the ordination of an openly non-celibate gay bishop could lead to a split in the church (and also in the worldwide Anglican Communion). I believe that the answers are related and lie in some ancient and modern history.

First, the ancient history. The Book of Leviticus was put together by the priestly authors of the Hebrew Scriptures in the seventh and sixth centuries BCE. Chapters 11 to 18 contain the laws of purity and the cultic procedures to be followed in dealing with defilement through unclean actions and contact with unclean things. These include childbirth, leprosy, bodily excretions and discharges, menstruation, and sexual intercourse, all of which render unclean those involved and thus required various cultic procedures for purification. (Many of these laws have parallels in other ancient Near Eastern religions.) The laws of purification were interpreted metaphorically or spiritualized in the New Testament, for example, in the phrase, purity of heart. William Countryman states that the New Testament writers shift between two quite different uses of purity language, literal and metaphorical as in purity of heart. He continues, "When the New Testament writers insist on purity as a standard of Christian conduct, they intend this latter, metaphorical sense. . . . With the possible exception of Jude and Revelation, all the [NT] documents that dealt with physical purity at all are agreed in rejecting it as an authoritative ethic for Christians as such. . . . Many modern Christians suppose that early Christians made a sharp distinction between purity rules touching on foods and those touching on sex, rejecting the former and retaining the latter. There is no justification for this position in the New Testament itself."[6]

Next, the modern history. In spite of the New Testament attitude toward these biblical passages about uncleanness and purification, they were sometimes interpreted literally and physically in Christian history but especially by the sects, in particular the Puritans of the seventeenth century and the Pietists of the eighteenth century. In Christianity the sect is originally a small group of Christians who retreat from the evil world to maintain its purity as against, for example, the national Church of England, which they described as a "mixed multitude." Countryman states: "A long history of pietism, both Protestant and Catholic, has made physical purity a major principle and sex a primary concern among us.... Pietism and revivalism made major contributions to the development and propagation of this purity code."[7] They longed for pure individuals in a pure church and applied a literal interpretation of the purity codes. Furthermore, H. Richard Niebuhr has argued that because of the influence of the frontier conditions, when the national churches of Europe came to America, they became sects, for example, the Polish National Catholic Church, and when the sects of Europe came to America they became great national churches, for example, the Baptists and the Methodists.[8] This is why the U. S. is probably the only nation in the world whose history of Christianity is largely sectarian in character. Most other nations have had national established churches. So sectarian Christianity has had a deep influence on American culture from the seventeenth century on into the present. I believe that this is a major source of our hysterical response to homosexuality.

Another aspect of the Puritan attitude toward homosexuality is its Calvinist understanding of God as unconditioned will who elects whom he will without any explanation. This is literally attested in God's word in the Bible. Any historical-critical questions about the Bible are irrelevant and even an indication that one is not a member of the elect. One's status as a member of the elect necessarily involves the distinction between

6. Countryman, *Dirt, Greed, and Sex*, 138–39.

7. Ibid., 142.

8. Niebuhr, *Social Sources of Denominationalism*, 145.

you and the non-elect, the heathen, the damned. Why then are homo-sexuals an important example of the non-elect? Probably because God is essentially symbolized in the Bible as male, as Father, Lord, and King. Therefore a chief symbol of God's relation to humanity is that of male to female, husband to wife. Since man is created in the image of God, any variation from this is clearly a departure from God's order of creation and thus to be condemned. It should be noted that it is almost always *male* homosexuality that triggers the hysteria we are discussing.[9] It seems that men can understand and accept female homosexuality for obvious reasons.

Some more of this history may illuminate the particular situation of the Episcopal Church in this hysteria. Among the churches of the Reformation of the sixteenth century the Church of England more than any other participated in the Renaissance tradition of historical criti-cal scholarship. For example, the great Renaissance scholar Desiderius Erasmus was a professor of Greek and New Testament at Cambridge University in the early sixteenth century. In the 1540s he published a new critical edition of the Greek text. He also published a book entitled *Paraphrases*, which was a commentary on all the New Testament books. The Archbishop of Canterbury required that this book be studied by all the clergy. Along with Erasmus there were also John Colet, Dean of St. Paul's, and Thomas More, the typical Renaissance man. So one of the main ingredients in the Anglicanism of the sixteenth century was this Renaissance tradition of the historical-critical interpretation of the Bible.

The main Anglican provinces who are suffering from this hysterical attitude toward homosexuality and the Episcopal Church's ordination of a non-celibate gay bishop are in Southeast Asia and especially Africa. Many of these churches were founded in the eighteenth centuries by missionaries sent out by the Church Missionary Society, a Pietist body that emphasized the literal interpretation of the King James version of the Bible published in 1611, and especially the purity codes of Leviticus and their apparent echoes in the New Testament. In seeking missionar-ies they claimed that they wanted not scholars but young men of faith. This interpretation of Scripture has been a major source of the hysteria over homosexuality coming from the Anglican churches of Africa and

9. See Charles Hefling, "How Shall We Know?" in Brown, *Other Voices, Other Worlds*, 81–99.

Asia. The Lambeth Conference of 1988 urges continuing discussion of the question of homosexuality including taking "account of biological, genetic, and psychological research . . . and the socio-cultural factors that lead to the different attitudes in the provinces of our Communion." This is yet to be done.

This raises the question of the nature of the alleged biblical condemnation of homosexual activity. The first point here is that the modern term "homosexuality" refers to sexual orientation, whereas the terminology that is alleged to refer to homosexual activity in the Bible referred in the minds of the authors to people whom they assumed, perhaps incorrectly, to be heterosexuals participating in homosexual acts that were considered to be degrading, especially because a man playing the role of a woman was the ultimate degradation in a strongly patriarchal society. Second, one of the main texts (which is also the origin of the term "sodomite") is Gen 19:1–11 in which the men of Sodom demand that Lot bring out his angelic guests so that they may "know" them. Many Old Testament scholars hold that the sin of the men of Sodom is primarily that of abuse of the sacred duty of hospitality, in Lot's case, against angelic guests.

Third, the main Greek terms referring to homosexuality are rare and vague. A very thorough recent study by a professor of New Testament at the (Jesuit) University of San Francisco, considers the Greek terms in 1 Cor 6:10, *malakoi* and *arsenokoitai*, which literally mean "soft" and "man-bed" and translated as "effeminate" and "abusers of themselves with mankind" in the King James Version with a reference to Lev 18:22. This study concludes:

> There has been and remains no consensus concerning the *meaning* of those terms, whether they involve sexual matters, let alone "homosexual" or same-sex activity, what activity or social relations the terms might imply, and what might qualify these activities as immoral. While many questions must remain open for lack of probative evidence, a few things are clear and certain. . . . Neither *malakoi* nor *arsenokoitai* can be translated with "homosexual," a term of modern coinage and shaped by modern conceptions of gender, gender identity, and sexual orientation (against the RSV 1946, TEV 1976, NEB 1971, NAB).[10]

10. See John H. Eliot, "Hunting for Homosexuals at Corinth," in McCaughey and Crocker, *From Biblical Interpretation to Human Transformation*, 29.

The Episcopal Church is confronted by a situation in which the Meeting of the Primates, or leaders of the thirty-eight provinces of the Anglican Communion, a group that came into being only in 1978, and has no real grounding in Anglican ecclesiology, has assumed the position of the highest authority in the Anglican Communion.[11] Now this body has issued a statement requesting "an unequivocal common covenant" that the House of Bishops of the Episcopal Church "will not authorize any Rite of Blessing for same-sex unions . . . [and] confirm . . . that a candidate for episcopal orders living in a same-sex union shall not receive the necessary consent." They warn that if this is not done, "The relationship between the Episcopal Church and the Anglican Communion as a whole remains damaged at best, and this has consequences for the full participation of the Church in the life of the Communion." Presumably at worst this would result in the excommunication of the Episcopal Church from the Anglican Communion.

The problems here are, first, that the House of Bishops cannot act for the Episcopal Church apart from the House of Deputies in General Convention, and, second, that neither the Primates Meeting nor any of the other Instruments of Unity of the Anglican Communion, namely, the Lambeth Conference of Bishops, the Archbishop of Canterbury, and the Anglican Consultative Council, has any authority to tell any of the Provinces what they must believe or do. The Instrument that has had the highest authority in the Communion, the Lambeth Conference of all the bishops of the Communion, has often declared that it has no such authority. The Lambeth Conference of 1998 calls upon the provinces to recognize "that there is and should be no compulsion on any bishop in matters concerning ordination or licensing." As Stephen Neill, (incidentally a gay bishop) in his fine work entitled *Anglicanism* has stated, "As has been repeatedly emphasized, the Lambeth Conference is neither a synod nor a council. None of its decisions or recommendations has any force in the life of any Province, unless it has been formally accepted by the Synod or General Council of that Province."[12] So unless the Episcopal Church can appeal the decision of the Primates Meeting to the next Lambeth Conference in 2008 on the complaint of a usurpation of authority on the part of the Primates, it must decide whether it will obey the Primates or

11. See L. William Countryman, "Politics, Polity, and the Bible as Hostage," in Linzey, *Gays and the Future of Anglicanism*, 2–16.

12. Neill, *Anglicanism*, 431.

follow the claim of the Gospel of Christ and perhaps be excommunicated from the Communion.

According to ethologists homosexuality is widespread in the animal kingdom, and according to various sociological studies between 4 to 10 percent of all humans are homosexual in orientation. This means that the Anglican churches have ordained thousands of homosexual priests and bishops during the last five hundred years. And it is probable that a large percent of them has not been celibate. So in effect the demand of the Primates is that gay priests and bishops should stay in or go back into the closet. It is a demand for hypocrisy rather than openness. Depending on the local circumstances these clergy have always had the choice of being in-the-closet or out-of-the closet depending on the local situation. The deepest closet has always been marriage and family. A gay Episcopal bishop friend and former colleague who lived in this deep closet all his ordained life finally decided to come out at his retirement. He knew six other bishops who were gay and all in the closet and asked them to come out with him, but they all turned him down

Change and progress in the Anglican Communion church has usually been accomplished by some province taking a new action rather than by the slow process of discussion, in all parishes, dioceses, provinces, and Instruments of Union, which would probably mean that any progress would be postponed indefinitely. This is perfectly illustrated in the case of women's ordination to the priesthood and episcopate, which was hastened by the irregular but valid ordination of eleven women priests in 1974 in which I particpated. In this connection the Lambeth Conference 1998 Resolution III.2 states, "This conference . . . calls upon the provinces of the Communion to uphold the principle of 'Open Reception' as it relates to the ordination of women to the priesthood as indicated by the Eames Commission; noting that 'reception is a long and spiritual process.'" It also calls upon the provinces "to affirm that those who dissent from, as well as those who assent to, the ordination of women to the priesthood and episcopate are both loyal Anglicans." Let us hope that the same may become the case in the ordination of non-celibate gay and lesbian people. This would constitute an appropriate example of doctrinal development and would require a theological argument based on the

Anglican theological criteria of Scripture, tradition, and reason in the classical Anglican tradition of Hooker, Sanderson, and Taylor.[13]

The diversity of state response to homosexual relations in the U. S. ranges from states that in 2007 declare same sex marriage and civil unions illegal to those in which it is legal, namely, Massachusetts, Connecticut, and New Jersey. This diversity is reflected in the situation in Africa where same-sex marriage is legal in South Africa and illegal in Nigeria and many other states. Nigeria is now considering a law in which five-year prison sentences would be imposed on those who have a same-sex marriage, and on those who perform it and those who attend it. It also criminalizes all political organizing and meetings on behalf of gay rights. This bill has the full and enthusiastic support of Archbishop Akinola of Nigeria, who is the ringleader of the hysteria over the ordination of a non-celibate gay bishop in the Episcopal Church. He claims that one of the reasons for his strong opposition to homosexuality is the pervasive cultural influence of strong Muslim opposition in Nigeria.

In the summer of 2007 I had the privilege of meeting with Mr. Davis Mac-Iyalla, a Nigerian who is the founder and Director of Changing Attitude Nigeria, a civil rights organization for homosexuals. Mr. Mac-Iyalla has been harassed, beaten, arrested, and the recipient of death threats for his work. He stated that he knows many homosexual Anglican bishops and priests in Nigeria, that there is little concern about homosexuality among Anglicans and Muslims in Nigeria, and that a Muslim leader had spoken publicly against the above-mentioned law. I asked him why Archbishop Akinola was carrying on his campaign in the United States, including the ordination of an American priest as bishop to minister to conservative parishes here, against strong request from the Archbishop of Canterbury to desist. He responded that he believed it was a power move to gain world-wide prestige, although Anglicans in Nigeria were largely unaware of his campaign. Archbishop Akinola obviously wants to be considered an African "Big Man."[14]

---

13. Charles Hefling has supplied an outline of such an argument in his essay, "A Reasonable Development?" in Linzey and Kirker, *Gays and the Future of Anglicanism*.

14. See Tangwa, *Road Companion to Democracy and Autocracy*, 78–79.

CHAPTER NINE

Prophecy and Politics: A Meditation

> WE LOOK FOR JUSTICE, but there is none; for salvation, but it is far
> from us. For our transgressions are multiplied before thee, and
> our sins testify against us: transgressing, and denying the Lord,
> and turning away from following our God. . . . Justice is turned
> back, and righteousness stands afar off; for truth has fallen in the
> public squares and uprightness cannot enter. . . . The Lord saw
> it, and it displeased him that there was no justice. . . . He put on
> righteousness as a breastplate, and a helmet of salvation upon his
> head; he put on garments of vengeance for clothing and wrapped
> himself in fury as a mantle. According to their deeds, so he will
> repay. . . . He will come to Zion as Redeemer, to those in Jacob
> who turn from transgression, says the Lord. (Isa 59:11–20)

The prophet Isaiah speaks the word of God to the people of Israel in the
late sixth century BCE. It is a hard time for the people of Israel. They are
still living under the heel of the Persians, although some are beginning to
return from exile to the ruins of Jerusalem. Therefore, the prophet's word
is one of lament that God's salvation is delayed, that the restoration of
Jerusalem has not yet come.

Says the prophet: "We wait for justice, but there is none; for salvation but it is far from us." And how does the prophet interpret this situation? The plight of Israel is the result of its sin, its injustice and idolatry.
"For our transgressions before you are many, and our sins testify against
us. Our transgressions indeed are with us, and we know our iniquities:
transgressing and denying the Lord, and turning away from following

116

our God. Justice is turned back, and righteousness stands at a distance; for truth stumbles in the public square, and uprightness cannot enter."

And what is God going to do about this, according to the prophet? God will come in judgment and salvation. "The Lord saw it and it displeased him that there was no justice. . . . He put on righteousness as a breastplate and a helmet of salvation on his head; he put on garments of vengeance for clothing and wrapped himself in fury as a mantle. According to their deeds he will repay" (Isa 59:15b–18a). But God comes in judgment only because God loves Israel and will also come as its savior. Says the prophet, "He will come to Zion as Redeemer, to those who turn from transgression says the Lord" (Isa 59:20).

So God calls the prophet to speak the word of God to the people of Israel in their national crisis of exile and destruction. Is there a word of God here for us today? Are we in a national crisis of destruction and exile? Apparently not at all. Indeed, if you listen to our political leaders, the state of the nation has never been better. Prosperity abounds, the Dow Jones hovering between thirteen and fourteen thousand, something unconceivable a few years ago, unemployment at an all time low, and so forth and so on. But what does the prophet say to this situation? Does God judge us as a nation on the basis of the Dow Jones, the Nasdaq, and the Gross Domestic Product? Not exactly.

The prophet says, "Justice is turned back and righteousness stands at a distance. . . . The Lord saw it and it displeased him that there was no justice." No, God judges the nation in regard to justice and righteousness. The overriding message of all the prophets is God's demand for justice, especially for the poor, the weak, and the vulnerable. And Jesus stood squarely in this prophetic tradition of the call for justice for the poor, the excluded, and the forgotten. In modern language we might summarize this as the call not for the economic health but for the *social* health of the nation. How are we doing in regard to social health? What do we hear about it in the media? Very little. And how can we find out about it? It is not easy. We are flooded with information about the economy. Every minute, hour, and day we are constantly updated not only on the Dow Jones and the Nasdaq, but also on the Standard and Poor's, the Index of Leading Economic Indicators, the Index of Consumer Confidence, and the Gross Domestic Product, all overseen by the Council of Economic Advisers to the President.

But how often do we hear about what are called the social indicators, the indicators of our social health as a nation, such as infant mortality, life expectancy, and so forth? Very rarely, only episodically, in local crises at most annually if you know where to look for it. There is no Index of Leading Social Indicators, very few reports, and no Council of Social Advisers to the President. (Almost all of the other advanced industrialized nations issue regular national social reports.) So how do we find out about the social health of our country? It just so happens that a few years ago a book was published entitled *The Social Health of the Nation: How America is Really Doing* by Marc and Marque-Luisa Miringoff, a couple of scholars at The Fordham Institute for Innovation in Social Policy.

They have analyzed sixteen social indicators over the last forty years, such as poverty, infant mortality, life expectancy, child abuse, youth suicide, average wages, teenage births and drug use, incarceration rate, and so forth. And what have they found? They have discovered that while the Gross Domestic Product has increased steadily over the past forty years, the average of the social indicators improved with the GDP until about 1970. Since then, while the GDP has increased 140 percent, the average of the social indicators has worsened 38 percent. It leveled off somewhat in the 1990s, but since then it has been plunging again. So today, the social health of our nation is poor and getting steadily worse. Some the indicators have improved and some have gone up and down, but the majority and the average have steadily worsened.

For example, when compared with the fifteen or twenty other developed or industrialized nations of the world, we are the highest in child poverty with 20 percent of all children living in poverty, the highest in youth homicide, the highest in teenage birth rate, the highest in income inequality, the highest in incarceration rate. We are very near the top in infant mortality and elder poverty. Thirty-seven million people in the United States are living in poverty. We are the lowest in high school graduation rate, near the bottom in life expectancy and thirteenth out of twenty-three in average hourly wages. We are the only Western industrialized nation without universal health care. There are forty-seven million people in the United States without any health insurance, including eight million children and twelve million veterans. We spend twice as much per capita on health care as any other nation, and we rank thirty-seventh in the world in the overall quality of our health care according to the World Health Organization.

So if God judges us as a nation on the basis our social health, then we are in serious trouble with God. Now, the prophet suggests that it is very dangerous to be in serious trouble with God. It means that judgment is coming, and that means that trouble is coming, for God is not mocked. This has been demonstrated over and over in human history, especially in the last century for those with eyes to see, the eyes of faith. So what does God through the prophet call us to do when we are in trouble with God? The prophet in this situation calls us to repentance and amendment of life. We know what repentance means. In regard to the social health of the nation it means primarily repentance for "what we have left undone." It means primarily sins of omission as well as sins of commission.

But what does amendment of life mean here? What can we do about the social health of the nation? What is our access to our national social health? Of course we can help with meals for the homeless and contribute to other programs for those in serious need. And these actions are very important. But they will not change the direction of the steady downward trend of our national social health.

I believe that our main access to the social health of the nation is through electoral politics. Isaiah was speaking the word of God to the people of Israel in a time of national crisis. It was political crisis of major proportions, the destruction of Jerusalem and exile in Babylon. As a matter of fact the Bible story is largely a story of politics, of national and international politics, a story of the struggles of peoples with kings, judges, and enemies.

But to consider the Bible as a political story sounds very odd. We generally look upon the Bible with reverence and admiration. That is not, however, the way we look at politics. As a nation we tend to look at politics and government with suspicion and disdain, even revulsion, or at best as entertainment. In the media today the word "politics" and its derivatives are always used pejoratively. Think of "politically correct," "politically motivated," to "politicize" something, to call someone "just a politician" or "very political," or refer to something as "just politics." They all have a negative connotation. In general, "politics" is something bad, corrupt, hopeless, and to be avoided.

A few years ago a book by Gary Wills was published with the title, *Necessary Evil: A History of the American Distrust of Government*. It is a history of the American suspicion and contempt for government from the nullifiers of the eighteenth century down to Timothy McVeigh's bombing of the federal building in Oklahoma City. We still hear of candidates running against the government, typified in Ronald Reagan's statement, "Government is not the solution; government is the problem."

Yet, all this negativity contradicts the grand Western tradition of the highest evaluation of politics. Plato began this tradition with his great work *The Republic*, and Aristotle continued it with his statement that we humans are political beings. The Greeks considered politics the most important subject of all. The *polis* is considered to be an association for leading the good life. The service of the *polis* was the highest human calling. So that not to be involved in politics is a diminishment of our being as humans.

I believe that our widespread negative attitude toward politics is an unconscious confession of our sin as a nation. Why? Because our politics is a perfect mirror of us as a nation. As a nation we get exactly the politics and government we deserve. Saint Augustine stated in one of his sermons, "Bad times, troublesome times, this is what men say. Let us live a good life, and the times are good. *We are the times*, such as we are, so are the times." We might say, "We are the times. Such as we are, so is our politics and our government."

But if electoral politics is the solution, the problem is that we are not using it. Less than one half of the eligible voters actually vote. Less than 30 percent of those between eighteen and twenty-four vote. And less than fifteen percent of the electorate does anything in politics beyond voting, which is the least form of our participation in politics. Among Western democracies we rank fifty-second out of fifty-eight in voter participation. This is why the social health of our nation is so poor. It is as simple as that.

This is where our amendment can begin. But amendment here is not as simple as giving up smoking, as difficult as that may be. Let me suggest what amendment here will mean. We must ask ourselves some very serious and demanding questions such as the following: Am I willing to run for public office, even for the school committee, or the city council, or even the state legislature, and so on? If not, am I willing to try to find and persuade some good candidates to run for these and other offices? If not, am I willing to campaign for the best candidates by volunteering for the various kinds of work involved in campaigns? If not, am I willing to contribute financially significant amounts to these campaigns? If not, am I willing at least to study the candidates, their qualifications and voting records, if any, as well as all the initiatives, in order to make educated judgments about which candidates and initiatives will do the most to improve the social health of the city, the county, the state, the nation, and the world? If not, am I willing at least to vote, the least of our responsibilities as citizens? If not, why am I surprised about the state of politics, government, and the social health of the nation? We are the times.

Democracy requires endless labor. As Jefferson said, "Eternal vigilance is the price of liberty." As we might put it, tireless effort is the price of democracy. And don't tell me about the much honored independent voters who are largely irrelevant to the political process and who in a recent study vote on the basis of personality rather than policy, on instinct rather than issues. We often hear people say that politics is hopelessly corrupt and that therefore that they will refuse to vote, and that is the best way to change the system. Please. I believe they know in their hearts that this is just a copout and they simply don't care. And why is it that politics is allegedly so corrupt as so many say? Because they do not participate.

So amendment of life is difficult here. It is very demanding. But I believe that it is our main calling today as Christians. Why? Because the fundamental principle of the Christian moral life is love of neighbor, and this means whole-hearted concern for the well-being of everyone whose life we can affect by our actions. And because of our democratic rights and processes and the power and influence of the United States in the world today, by our actions as citizens in electoral politics we affect the lives of not only everyone in our nation but also everyone in the whole world. So love of neighbor sends us into politics. Not long ago the Roman Catholic bishops sent a statement to all their parishes stating, "Participation in the political process is a moral responsibility." Amen to that. God has given our nation and its social health and indeed the whole world, our very history, into our hands. So a terrible responsibility rests upon us today, a responsibility for amendment of life and full participation in the political process of our nation, to move it toward greater social health and the world toward greater justice and peace.

Thus the message of the prophet is that God comes to us in judgment and salvation. Why? Because God loves us and cares about how we live, and longs to lead us to our fulfillment. Because God loves us with an intensity and steadfastness we can barely grasp, a love shown to us in our savior Jesus Christ. This is why God calls us to repentance and amendment of life, to thanksgiving for our blessings, and to the rededication of our lives to God's service in the struggle for justice and peace in our nation and the world.

APPENDIX: ACTIVIST, MOVEMENT, AND THIRD-PARTY POLITICS

A TIDAL MOVEMENT IN progressive politics in the last four decades has produced a sea change in the United States and has led to the ascendancy of the radical right. This tidal movement consists of the retreat of progressives from major party electoral politics into non-electoral activist, movement, and third party politics all of which show the same mentality.[1] This began in the anti-war movement of the late 1960s. Previous movements such as the labor and civil rights movements had no alternative to activism in the form of demonstrations, but they had electoral and legal goals. The participants in the anti-war movement had an alternative, namely, electoral politics. But they were outraged by the nomination of Humphrey who, they believed, would continue Johnson's war; and therefore they concluded that electoral politics was hopeless. So they rioted in Chicago, thus alienating many of the electorate, and decided to sit out the election thus leading to the victory of Nixon who extended the Vietnam War for five years and founded the Rehnquist court. In other words, they achieved the opposite of their goals. This was the beginning of non-electoral activist and movement politics, and third party politics shares the same mentality. Let us consider these phenomena, beginning with the last.

Third parties, or more accurately non-major parties, have been a factor in U. S. politics since the 1830s when the Anti-Masonic Party emerged, but they have usually not lasted very long. Since 1948 there have been presidential candidates of eighty-one non-major parties on the ballot, but their average longevity has been only two election cycles. Fifty-two of the eighty-one have been on the presidential ballot only once.

Occasionally, however, they have been critical. In 1856 the Republican Party replaced the Whigs as a major party in the crisis over slavery. In 1912 Theodore Roosevelt, after losing the Republican nomination to William Howard Taft, ran as the Progressive Bull Moose candidate and delivered the election to Democrat Woodrow Wilson. Then in November 2003 John Miller of *The National Review* noted in *The New York Times*

1. See Rorty, *Achieving Our Country*, ch. 1.

that there have been three consecutive elections in which a Libertarian candidate has cost the Republican Party a seat in the Senate. He then stated, "George W. Bush is president today because of Ralph Nader," referring to the fact that Nader took enough votes away from Gore to give the electoral votes of Florida, New Hampshire, and Tennessee to Bush. Exit polls in that election indicated that 80 percent of Nader voters would have voted for Gore if Nader had not been on the ballot. This was predicted by Gary Trudeau's comic strip Doonesbury on election day 2000 when he tried to alert his Green readers and others to this fact of political life: "If you'd like to see abortion recriminalized, if you're for unrestrained logging and drilling and for voluntary pollution control, if you favor more soft money in politics, then the choice today is clear . . . Vote Nader." Miller concludes, "Libertarians are now serving, in effect, as Democratic Party operatives." And he could have added that Greens have been serving, in effect, as Republican Party operatives. He could also have noted that we now know that in 2000, Republican campaigners actually served as Green Party operatives in at least two states. The third party issue arises again in the 2008 campaigns because of the possible candidacy of the billionaire former Republican, now Independent, mayor of New York, Michael Bloomberg.

I have often wondered why it is that people vote for third parties or participate in non-electoral activist and movement politics, when they know, or should know if they thought about it, that such as this will usually accomplish the opposite of their objectives. If that is the case, why do they do it? In an essay in *The Nation* in 2001 the actor Tim Robbins explained why he voted for Nader: "I would rather vote my conscience than vote strategically." Throughout the essay he emphasizes the fundamental importance of ideals, idealism, vision, passion, dreams, heart, and following one's inner voice. He condemns voting strategically, compromising one's ideals or one's integrity, and voting for the lesser of two evils. He obviously has not had enough political experience to realize that all important political achievements have always involved strategic planning and action, making compromises in order to build coalitions, and voting for the lesser of two evils, or better put, for the better of two imperfect candidates or pieces of legislation. Rorty has put it this way: "In democratic countries you get things done by compromising your principles in order to form alliances with groups about whom you have grave doubts."[2] Robbins fears that participating in this kind of politics would involve giving up his ideals, his integrity, his vision, his dreams, his inner voice, and violating his conscience, whereas someone who understands politics would affirm that participating in this kind of politics constitutes the only way to fulfill all these values. Although I sometimes agree more with the platform of the Green Party than with that of the Democratic Party, I am not persuaded by Robbins's flawed moral argument.

I got a clue to the answer to my question about why people vote for third party candidates when I reread Max Weber's famous 1919 essay entitled "Politics as a Vocation." In it he distinguishes between two views of ethics that are applied to politics. He calls them the "ethic of ultimate ends" (a better translation is the ethic of intention), which emphasizes purity of motive or attitude, and the "ethic of responsibility," which stresses consequences, "the foreseeable results of one's action." Weber concludes that the only ethic that has any place in politics is the ethic of responsibility focused on consequences. He writes, "Anyone who fails to see this is, indeed, a political infant." He continues,

> You may demonstrate to a convinced syndicalist, believing in an ethic of ultimate ends, that his action will result in increasing the opportunities of reaction, in increasing the oppression of his class, and obstructing its ascent—and you will not make the slightest impression upon him. If an action of good intent leads to bad results, then in the actor's eyes, not he but the world, or the stupidity of other men . . . is responsible for the evil. . . . The believer in an ethic of ultimate ends feels "responsible" only for seeing to it that the flame of pure intentions is not quenched: for example, the flame of protesting against the injustice of the social order. To rekindle the flame ever anew is the purpose of his quite irrational deeds, judged in view of their possible success.[3]

I believe that third party voters tend to be committed to the ethic of intention, the ethic of purity of motive. They believe that if they act with purity of intention they have fulfilled their responsibility and if this does not produce the expected results, then that is the fault of something or someone else. For example, after the 2000 election there was a letter in a progressive religious journal complaining that there must be some-

2. Rorty, *Achieving Our Country*, 52.
3. Weber, *Politics as a Vocation*, 47.

thing wrong with our political system because when the author "voted [his] conscience" (presumably Nader) he was "rewarded with [his] worst nightmare" (presumably Bush). According to Weber, the Greens should have asked themselves in 2000 this question: a vote for which candidate will result in the best consequences for the environment: Bush, who is deeply committed to the fossil fuels industries, Nader, who has no chance of being elected, or Gore, the most environmentally informed and committed of any candidate in the past century?

This indifference to consequences is not a new phenomenon. It was illustrated in the career of Percy Bysshe Shelley, the great Romantic poet of the early nineteenth century who claimed to be a great activist in the cause of human rights. In his review of a new book about Shelley, Adam Kirsch states,

> There is something exasperating, or worse, about the idea of Shelley about trying to change the world with toy balloons [a reference to his sending balloons containing his pamphlet "A Declaration of Human Rights" toward Wales and Ireland]. Throughout his adulthood he considered himself a serious radical—even claiming, 'I consider poetry very subordinate to moral and political science'—whose purpose was to advance the cause of liberty in England and Europe. But he consistently displayed an indifference to reality which went deeper than his propaganda techniques. Shelley's ineffectiveness as an agitator we could dismiss with a smile. But his political beliefs demonstrated the same contempt of consequence, the same elevation of pure motive over practical effects, the same lack of self-awareness. These qualities helped to make Shelley a genuinely illiberal thinker, whole politics verged at times on the totalitarian.[4]

Where then does this deep concern for purity of motive and intention come from? In the United States, at least, I believe it comes from a deep cultural undercurrent that is derived from the ethos of seventeenth-century Puritans and eighteenth-century Pietists and originally from the Bible, and it focuses on personal purity of heart and intention. I am not suggesting that that all third party voters are Puritans or Pietists, but that they are the inheritors of a deep and pervasive religious cultural tradition of purity of heart and intention.

4. Kirsch, "Avenging Angel: Inside Shelley's Manichaean Mind," 85–86.

Sharing the same spirit with that of third party politics is movement politics or "activism," which, as noted above, in its current form arose in the late 1960s in connection with the anti-war movement. Movement politics and activism suggest another interpretation of the spirit shared with third party politics: fantasy. This interpretation was offered in 2002 by Lee Harris in an essay in *Policy Review* on what he calls "fantasy ideology." He tells of a fellow graduate student in the late 1960s who as an antiwar protest joined many others in lying down on the bridges over the Potomac River in Washington in order to disrupt traffic. When Harris pointed out to his friend that this action was ineffective, counterproductive, and thus politically irresponsible, he responded that this was entirely irrelevant. When Harris then inquired as to why he was doing it, he responded that it was "good for his soul." Harris continues, "What I saw as a political act was not, for my friend, any such thing. It was not aimed at altering the minds of other people or persuading them to act differently. Its whole point was what it did for *him*. And what it did for him was to provide him with a fantasy—a fantasy, namely, of taking part in the revolutionary struggle of the oppressed against their oppressors."[5]

A fine fictional picture of the spirit and irrelevance of such activism has been presented by Doris Lessing in her novel *The Good Terrorist* in which a woman is talking with her friend:

> "What have we got in common now? We've been cooking meals and talking about our bloody children, and going on demonstrations."
>
> "I haven't noticed you going on any recently."
>
> "No, not since I understood that demos and all that are just for *fun*."
>
> "For fun are they?"
>
> "Yes, that's right. People go on demos because they get a kick out of it. Like picnics."
>
> "You can't be serious, Dorothy."
>
> "Of course I'm serious. No one bothers to ask any longer if it achieves anything, going on marches or demos. They talk about how they feel. That's what they care about. It's for kicks. It's for *fun*."
>
> "Dorothy, that's simply perverse."
>
> "Why is it perverse if it's true? You've just got to use your eyes and look—people picketing, or marching or demonstrating, they

5. Harris, "Al Quaeda's Fantasy Ideology," 3.

are having a marvelous time. And if they are beaten by the police, so much the better. . . . I'll tell you something, Zoë. All you people, marching up and down and waving banners and singing pathetic little songs—'All You Need is Love'—you are just a joke. To the people who really run the world, you are a joke. They watch you at it and think: Good, that's keeping them busy."[6]

Harris' point about fantasy probably has its origin in the fact that we in the United States and Britain are involved in a new Romantic movement. Craig Brinton describes the Romantic temperament as "eager for novelty, for adventure, above all for the vicarious adventure of fantasy."[7] Nader's campaigns have drawn on the current Romantic movement especially in its emphasis on the heroic individual struggling against the vast corporate forces of evil and thus on the fantasy of participating in a movement that would transform American society.

This means that devotees of activist, movement, and third party politics should try to overcome their obsession with purity of intention and fantasy, and with a politically informed intention and conscience put their efforts into changing the direction of the major party nearest to their own policy convictions by investing their energy, time, talents, and resources into its primaries and campaigns. This will indeed be much more effective in achieving their goals.

6. Lessing, *The Good Terrorist*, 412–13.
7. For the details, see chapter 3.

BIBLIOGRAPHY

Aburdene, Patricia. *Megatrends 2070: The Rise of Conscious Capitalism*. Charlottesville: Hampton Roads, 2005.

Ahlstrom, Sydney E. "Romanticism as a Religious Revolution." Unpublished essay.

Allen, Diogenes. *Spiritual Theology: A Theology of Yesterday for Spiritual Help Today*. Cambridge, MA: Cowley, 1997.

Barth, Karl. *Church Dogmatics*. 13 vols. Translated by G. W Bromiley et al. Edinburgh: T. & T. Clark, 1956–1975.

Bayne, Stephen F. Jr., editor. *Theological Freedom and Social Responsibility*. New York: Seabury, 1967.

Bellah, Robert, et al. *Habits of the Heart: Individualism and Commitment in American Life*. New York: Harper & Row, 1985.

Benhabib, Seyla. *Situating the Self: Gender, Community, and Postmodernism in Contemporary Ethics*. New York: Routledge, 1992.

Benn, S. I., and Gerald F. Gauss, editors. *Public and Private in Social Life*. New York: St. Martin's, 1983.

Best, Steven, and Douglas Kellner. *The Postmodern Turn*. New York: Guilford, 1997.

Bloom, Harold. *The American Religion: The Emergence of the Post-Christian Nation*. New York: Simon & Schuster, 1992.

———. *Omens of the Millennium: The Gnosis of Angels, Dreams, and Resurrection*. New York: Riverhead, 1996.

Booker, Christopher. *The Neophiliacs: A Study of the Revolution in English Life in the Fifties and Sixties*. London: Collins, 1969.

The Book of Common Prayer. New York: The Church Hymnal Corporation, 1979.

Brinton, Craig. "Romanticism." In *The Encyclopedia of Philosophy*, 7:206–9. 8 vols. New York: Macmillan, 1967.

Brown, Terry, editor. *Other Voices, Other Worlds. The Global Church Speaks Out on Homosexuality*. New York: Hunt, 2005.

Bultmann, Rudolph. *Theology of the New Testament*. 2 vols. New York: Scribner's, 1948–1953.

————, et al. *Kerygma and Myth: A Theological Debate*. Edited by Hans Werner Bartsch. New York: Harper, 1962.

Burton-Christie, Douglas. "Retrieval." *Spiritus: A Journal of Christian Spirituality* 3:2 (2003) vii–ix.

Buttrick, David. *Homiletic: Moves and Structures*. Philadelphia: Fortress, 1987.

Calvin, John. *Theological Treatises*. Translated with introduction and notes by J. K. S. Reid. Philadelphia: Westminster, 1954.

Campbell, Colin. *The Romantic Ethic and the Spirit of Modern Consumerism*. Oxford: Blackwell, 1987.

Carrette, Jeremy, and Richard King. *Selling Spirituality: The Silent Takeover of Religion*. London: Routledge, 2005.

Cassirer, Ernst. *The Platonic Renaissance in England*. Translated by James P. Pettegrove. Austin: University of Texas Press, 1953.

Chandler, Stuart. "When the World Falls Apart: Method for Employing Chaos and Emptiness as Theological Constructs." *Harvard Theological Review* 85 (1992) 467–91.

Cherbonnier, Edmond La B. "Is There a Biblical Metaphysic?" *Theology Today* 15 (1959) 454–69.

Church of England. *Certain Sermons or Homilies Appointed to be Read in Churches*. Oxford: Clarendon, 1822.

Cooke, Bernard. *Ministry to Word and Sacraments: History and Theology*. Philadelphia: Fortress, 1976.

Countryman, L. William. *Dirt, Greed, and Sex: Sexual Ethics in the New Testament and their Implications for Today*. Philadelphia: Fortress, 1988.

Cousins, Ewert, editor. *World Spirituality: An Encyclopedic History of the Religious Quest*. New York: Crossroad, 1985.

Crabtree, Davida Foy. *The Empowering Church: How One Congregation Supports Lay People's Ministries in the World*. Washington DC: Alban Institute, 1989.

Crossman, R. H. S., editor. *The God that Failed: Six Studies in Communism*. London: Hamilton, 1950.

Denziger, Heinrich. *The Sources of Catholic Dogma*. Translated by Roy R. Deferrari. St. Louis: Herder, 1957.

Dewey, John. *A Common Faith*. New Haven: Yale University Press, 1934.

Douglas, Ann. *The Feminization of American Culture*. New York: Knopf, 1977.

Downey, Michael. *Understanding Christian Spirituality*. New York: Paulist, 1992.

Drees, C. A. "Platonism and the Platonic Tradition." In *The Encyclopedia of Philosophy*, 8:333–41. New York: Macmillan, 1967.

Drury, Shadia. *Alexandre Kojève: The Roots of Postmodern Politics*. New York: St. Martin's, 1994.

————. *Leo Strauss and the American Right*. New York: St. Martin's, 1997.

————. *The Political Ideas of Leo Strauss: Updated Edition*. New York: Macmillan, 2005.

Dudley, Carl S., editor. *Building Effective Ministry: Theory and Practice in the Local Church*. San Francisco: Harper & Row, 1983.

Evans, H. Barry. "Introduction." *Anglican Theological Review* 62 (1980) 195–96.

Fenhagen, James C. *Ministry for a New Time: Case Study for Change.* Washington DC: Alban Institute, 1995.

Fitzmyer, Joseph A. *The Gospel According to Luke.* Anchor Bible 28–28A. Garden City, NY: Doubleday, 1981–1985.

Fleischner, Eva, editor. *Auschwitz, Beginning of a New Era? Reflections on the Holocaust: Papers Given at the International Symposium on the Holocaust, Held at the Cathedral of Saint John the Divine, New York City, June 3 to 6, 1974.* New York: KTAV, 1977.

Forstman, Jack. *A Romantic Triangle: Schleiermacher and Early German Romanticism.* Missoula: Scholars, 1970.

Fromm, Erich. "Problems of Surplus." In *The Essential Fromm: Life Between Having and Being,* edited by Rainer Funk. New York: Continuum, 1995.

Fuller, Robert C. *Spiritual, but Not Religious: Understanding Unchurched America.* Oxford: Oxford University Press, 2001.

Goethe, Johann Wolfgang von. *The Autobiography of Johann Wolfgang von Goethe.* Translated by John Oxenford. New York: Horizon, 1969.

Harris, Lee. "Al Quaeda's Fantasy Ideology." *Policy Review* 114 (2002).

Hefner, Philip. "God and Chaos: The Demiurge versus the Ungrund." *Zygon* 19 (1984) 469–85.

Heim, Karl. *Christian Faith and Natural Science.* Translated by N. Horton Smith. New York: Harper, 1953.

Hillman, James, and Michael Ventura. *We've Had a Hundred Years of Psychotherapy—And the World's Getting Worse.* New York: HarperCollins, 1992.

Holifield, E. Brooks. "The Historian and the Congregation." In *Beyond Clericalism: The Congregation as a Focus of Theological Education,* edited by Joseph C. Hough Jr. and Barbara G. Wheeler. Atlanta: Scholars, 1988.

Holmes, Urban T. "Theology and Religious Renewal." *Anglican Theological Review* 62 (1980) 3–19.

Hough, Joseph C. Jr., and Barbara G. Wheeler, editors. *Beyond Clericalism: The Congregation as a Focus for Theological Education.* Atlanta: Scholars, 1988.

Huchingson, James E. *Pandemonium Tremendum: Chaos and Mystery in the Life of God.* Cleveland: Pilgrim, 2001.

Inge, William Ralph. *The Philosophy of Plotinus: The Gifford Lectures at St. Andrews.* 3rd ed. London: Longmans, Green, 1948.

———. *The Platonic Tradition in English Religious Thought: The Hulsean Lectures at Cambridge, 1925–1928.* New York: Longmans, Green, 1926.

Jackson, Kenneth T. *Crabgrass Frontier: The Suburbanization of the United States.* New York: Oxford University Press, 1985.

Jones, W. T. *The Romantic Syndrome: Toward a New Method in Cultural Anthropology and History of Ideas.* The Hague: Martins Nijhoff, 1961.

Keating, Thomas *Open Mind, Open Heart: The Contemplative Dimension of the Gospel.* New York: Continuum, 1999.

Keble, John. *The Works of the Learned and Judicious Mr. Richard Hooker.* 2 vols. New York: Appleton, 1890.

Kegley, Charles W., and Robert Bretall. *The Theology of Paul Tillich*. New York: Macmillan, 1952.

Keller, Catherine. *Face of the Deep: A Theology of Becoming*. New York: Routledge, 2003.

Kerr, Fergus. *Theology After Wittgenstein*. Oxford: Blackwell, 1986.

Kirk, Kenneth E. *The Vision of God: The Christian Doctrine of the Summum Bonum*. London: Longmans, Green, 1932.

Kirsch, Adam. "Avenging Angel: Inside Shelley's Manichaean Mind." *New Yorker*, August 27, 2007, 85–86.

Kraemer, Hendrik. *A Theology of the Laity*. Philadelphia: Westminster, 1958.

Leith, John, editor. *Creeds of the Churches: A Reader in Christian Doctrine from the Bible to the Present*. Garden City, NY: Doubleday, 1963.

Lessing, Doris. *The Good Terrorist*. New York: Vantage, 1985.

———. *Theories of Preaching: Selected Readings in the Homiletical Tradition*. Durham, NC: Labyrinth, 1987.

Lindbeck, George A. *The Nature of Doctrine: Religion and Theology in a Postliberal Age*. Philadelphia: Westminster, 1984.

Linzey, Andrew, and Richard Kirker, editors. *Gays and the Future of Anglicanism: Responses to the Windsor Report*. New York: Hunt, 2005.

Lischer, Richard. *A Theology of Preaching: The Dynamics of the Gospel*. Nashville: Abingdon, 1981.

———, editor. *Theories of Preaching: Selected Readings in the Homiletical Tradition*. Durham, NC: Labyrinth, 1987.

Locklin, Reid B. *Spiritual but Not Religious? An Oar Stroke Closer, to the Farther Shore*. Collegeville: Liturgical, 2005.

Long, Thomas, and Edward Farley, editors. *Preaching as a Theological Task: World, Gospel, Scripture: In Honor of David Buttrick*. Louisville: Westminster John Knox, 1996.

Mabry, John R. "The Gnostic Generation: Understanding and Ministering to Generation X." *Presence: The Journal of Spiritual Directors International* 5:2 (1999) 35–47.

MacIntyre, Alasdair. *After Virtue: A Study in Moral Theory*. Notre Dame: University of Notre Dame Press, 1984.

Macquarrie, John. *Principles of Christian Theology*. New York: Scribner's, 1966.

Maguire, Meredith. "Mapping Contemporary American Spirituality." *Christian Spirituality Bulletin* 5 (1997) 3–8.

Martin, Bernice. *A Sociology of Contemporary Cultural Change*. New York: St. Martin's, 1981.

Marty, Martin E. *The Public Church: Mainline—Evangelical—Catholic*. New York: Crossroad, 1981.

McCaughey, Douglas R., and Cornelia Cyss Crocker, editors. *From Biblical Interpretation to Human Transformation*. Salem, OR: Chora Strangers, 2006.

McCord, James I. "Editorial: The Blurred Vision." *Theology Today* 28 (1971) 271–77.

Moore, Paul Elmer, and Frank Cross. *Anglicanism: The Thought and Practice of the Church of England, Illustrated From the Literature of the Seventeenth Century.* London: SPCK, 1951.

Muirhead, John H. *The Platonic Tradition in Anglo-Saxon Philosophy: Studies in the History of Idealism in England and America.* London: Allen & Unwin 1965.

Musgrove, Frank. *Ecstasy and Holiness: Counter Culture and the Open Society.* Bloomington: Indiana University Press, 1974.

Neill, Stephen. *Anglicanism.* Baltimore: Penguin, 1958.

Newbigin, Lesslie. *The Household of God: Lectures on the Nature of the Church.* London: SCM, 1953.

Newman, John Henry, John Keble, William Palmer, Richard Hurrell Froude, E. B. Pusey, and Isaac Williams. *Tracts for the Times.* 2 vols. London: Rivington, 1840–42.

Nichols, J. Randall. "What is the Matter with the Teaching of Preaching?" *Anglican Theological Review* 62 (1980) 221–38.

Nicholson, Linda J., editor. *Feminism/Postmodernism.* New York: Routledge, 1990.

Niebuhr, H. Richard. *The Social Sources of Denominationalism.* New York: Meridian, 1957.

Ó Murchú, Diarmuid. *Religion in Exile: A Spiritual Vision for the Homeward Bound.* Dublin: Gateway, 2000.

O'Regan, Cyril. *Gnostic Apocalypse: Jacob Boehme's Haunted Narrative.* Albany: State University of New York Press, 2002.

———. *Gnostic Return in Modernity.* Albany: State University of New York Press, 2001.

Outler, Albert C., editor. *John Wesley.* New York: Oxford University Press, 1964.

Paradise, Scott I. *Detroit Industrial Mission: A Personal Narrative.* New York: Harper & Row, 1968.

Pennington, M. Basil. *Centering Prayer: Renewing an Ancient Christian Prayer Form.* New York: Doubleday, 1980.

Phillips, Jennifer M. "Same-Sex Unions." *The Witness* 77:12 (1994).

Pike, James A., editor. *Modern Canterbury Pilgrims: And Why They Chose the Episcopal Church.* New York: Morehouse-Gorham, 1956.

Pittenger, Norman. "Paul Tillich as a Theologian: An Appreciation." *Anglican Theological Review* 43 (1961) 268–86.

Polenberg, Richard. *One Nation Divisible: Class, Race, and Ethnicity in the United States Since 1938.* New York: Penguin, 1980.

Putnam, Robert D. *Bowling Alone: The Collapse and Revival of American Community.* New York: Simon & Schuster, 2000.

Reade, W. H. V. *The Christian Challenge to Philosophy.* London: SPCK, 1958.

Ricoeur, Paul. *The Symbolism of Evil.* Translated by Emerson Buchanan. Boston: Beacon, 1967.

Rieff, Philip. *The Triumph of the Therapeutic: The Uses of Faith After Freud.* New York: Harper & Row, 1966.

Reitz, Rudiger. *The Church in Experiment: Studies in New Congregational Structures and Functional Mission.* Nashville: Abingdon, 1968.

Roberts, Alexander, James Donaldson, and A. Cleveland Coxe. *Ante-Nicene Fathers: The Writings of the Fathers Down to A.D. 325*. 10 vols. Peabody: Hendrickson, 1995.

Roof, Wade Clark. *Spiritual Marketplace: Baby Boomers and the Remaking of American Religion*. Princeton: Princeton University Press, 1999.

Roozen, David A., William McKinney, and Jackson W. Carroll. *Varieties of Religious Presence: Mission in Public Life*. New York: Pilgrim, 1984.

Rorty, Richard. *Achieving Our Country: Leftist Thought in Twentieth-Century America*. Cambridge: Harvard University Press, 1998.

Roszak, Theodore. *The Making of a Counter Culture: Reflections on the Technocratic Society and Its Youthful Opposition*. Garden City: Doubleday, 1969.

—————. *Where the Wasteland Ends: Politics and Transcendence in Postindustrial Society*. Garden City: Doubleday, 1972.

Rowell, Geoffrey, Kenneth Stevenson, and Rowan Williams, editors. *Love's Redeeming Work: The Anglican Quest for Holiness*. Oxford: Oxford University Press, 2001.

Rowthorn, Anne W. *The Liberation of the Laity*. Wilton, CT: Morehouse-Barlow, 1986.

Russell, Robert John, Nancey Murphy, and Arthur R. Peacocke, editors. *Chaos and Complexity: Scientific Perspectives on Divine Action*. Berkeley: The Center for Theology and the Natural Sciences, 1995.

Ryan, Michael D. "The New Romanticism and Biblical Faith." In *Auschwitz: Beginning of a New Era? Reflections on the Holocaust: Papers given at the International Symposium on the Holocaust, held at the Cathedral of Saint John the Divine, New York City, June 3 to 6, 1974*, edited by Eva Fleischner. New York: KM, 1977.

Sample, Tex. *U. S. Lifestyles and Mainline Churches: A Key to Reaching People in the 90's*. Louisville: Westminster John Knox, 1990.

Schneiders, Sandra M. "Religion vs. Spirituality: A Contemporary Conundrum." *Spiritus: A Journal of Christian Spirituality* 3 (2003) 163–65.

Schor, Juliet. *The Commercialized Child and the New Consumer Culture*. New York: Scribner, 2004.

—————. *Do Americans Shop Too Much?* Boston: Beacon, 2000.

—————, and Douglas B. Holt, editors. *The Consumer Society Reader*. New York: New Press, 2000.

Shand-Tucci, Douglass. *Ralph Adams Cram: Life and Architecture*. Amherst: University of Massachusetts Press, 1995.

Shannon, William A. *Silent Lamp: The Thomas Merton Story*. New York: Crossroad, 1992.

Shepherd, Massey Hamilton Jr. *The Oxford American Prayer Book Commentary*. New York: Oxford University Press, 1950.

Smith, Huston. *Forgotten Truth: The Primordial Tradition*. New York: Harper & Row, 1976.

Smith, Martin L. *A Season for the Spirit*. Cambridge, MA: Cowley, 1991.

—————. *The Word Is Very Near You: A Guide To Praying With Scripture*. Cambridge, MA: Cowley, 1989.

Snow, John. "Reflections on Anglican Preaching." *Anglican Theological Review* 62 (1980) 211–20.

Sobrino, Jon. *Spirituality of Liberation: Toward a Political Holiness.* Maryknoll, NY: Orbis, 1988.

Society of St. John the Evangelist. *The Rule of the Society of Saint John the Evangelist.* Cambridge, MA: Cowley, 1997.

Stendahl, Krister. "Biblical Theology." In *Interpreter's Dictionary of the Bible,* edited by Keith Crim, 1:418–32. New York: Abingdon, 1962.

Sykes, Stephen, and John Booty, editors. *The Study of Anglicanism.* London: SPCK, 1988.

Tangwa, Godfrey B. *Road Companion to Democracy and Autocracy: Further Essays from an African Perspective.* Bellingham, WA: Kola Tree, 1998.

Taylor, Brian C. *Becoming Christ: Transformation Through Contemplation.* Cambridge, MA: Cowley, 2002.

Taylor, Charles. *Sources of the Self: The Making of the Modern Identity.* Cambridge: Harvard University Press, 1989.

Taylor, Jeremy. *The Rule and Exercises of Holy Living.* 1650. Reprint: Eugene, OR: Wipf & Stock, 2007.

———. *The Rule and Exercises of Holy Dying.* 1651. Reprint: London: Dutton, 1876.

Temple, William. *Christian Faith and Life.* London: Mowbray, 1931.

———. *Christianity and Social Order.* New York: Seabury, 1977.

———. *Christus Veritas.* New York: MacMillan, 1925.

———. "Chairman's Introduction." In *Doctrine in the Church of England.* London: SPCK, 1938.

———. *Nature, Man and God.* London: Macmillan, 1934.

Thiselton, Anthony C. *The Two Horizons: New Testament Hermeneutics and Philosophical Description with Special Reference to Heidegger, Bultmann, Gadamer, and Wittgenstein.* Grand Rapids: Eerdmans, 1980.

Thomas Aquinas. *Summa Theologica.* 5 vols. Translated by Fathers of the English Dominican Province. Allen, TX: Christian Classics, 1981.

Thomas, Owen C. "Chaos, Complexity, and God: A Review Essay." *Theology Today* 54 (1997) 66–76.

———. "Interiority and Christian Spirituality." *The Journal of Religion* 80 (2000) 41–60.

———. "Political Spirituality: Oxymoron or Redundancy?" *Journal of Religion and Society* 3 (2001) 1–12.

———. "Public Theology and Counter-Public Spheres." *Harvard Theological Review* 85 (1992) 453–69.

———. *Theological Questions: Analysis and Argument.* Wilton, CT: Morehouse-Barlow, 1983.

———. *What Is it that Theologians Do, How they Do it, and Why: Anglican Essays.* Lewiston, NY: Edwin Mellen, 2006.

———, and Ellen K. Wondra. *Introduction to Theology.* 3rd ed. Harrisburg, PA: Morehouse, 2002.

Thompsett, Fredrica Harris. *We Are Theologians: Strengthening the People of the Episcopal Church.* Cambridge, MA: Cowley, 1989.

Thornton, Martin. *English Spirituality: An Outline of Ascetical Theology According to the English Pastoral Tradition.* Cambridge, MA: Cowley, 1986.

Tillich, Paul. *Systematic Theology.* 3 vols. Chicago: University of Chicago Press, 1951–1963.

———. *Theology of Culture.* Edited by Robert C. Kimball. New York: Oxford University Press, 1959.

Van Buren, Paul M. "The Word of God in the Church." *Anglican Theological Review* 39 (1957) 344–58.

Van Ness, Peter H. *Spirituality and the Secular Quest.* Vol. 22 of *World Spirituality: An Encylopedic History of the Religious Qeust,* edited by Ewert Cousins. New York: Crossroad, 1996.

Vidler, A. R. *Essays in Liberality.* London: SCM, 1957.

———, editor. *Soundings: Essays Concerning Christian Understanding.* Cambridge: Cambridge University Press, 1962.

Wakefield, Gordon S. "Anglican Spirituality." In *Christian Spirituality: Post Reformation and Modern.* Vol. 18 in *World Spirituality: An Encyclopedic History of the Religious Quest,* edited by Louis Dupré and Don E. Saliers, 257–93. New York: Crossroad, 1996.

Weber, Max. *Politics as a Vocation.* Translated by H. H. Gerth and C. Wright Mills. Philadelphia: Fortress, 1965.

Welsh, Clement W. "Preaching as Apologetics." *Anglican Theological Review* 62 (1980) 239–52.

Wesley, John. *The Works of John Wesley.* Edited by Albert C. Outler. 14 vols. Nashville: Abingdon, 1984.

Wickham, Edward Ralph. *Church and People in an Industrial City.* London: Lutterworth, 1957, 1969.

Willimon, William H. *Pastor: The Theology and Practice of Ordained Ministry.* Nashville: Abingdon, 2002.

Wilson, Paul Scott. *The Four Pages of a Sermon: A Guide to Biblical Preaching.* Nashville: Abingdon, 1999.

Winter, Gibson. *The New Creation as Metropolis.* New York: Macmillin, 1963.

———. *The Suburban Captivity of the Churches: An Analysis of Protestant Responsibility in the Expanding Metropolis.* Garden City: Doubleday, 1961.

Wolf, William J., editor. *Anglican Spirituality.* Wilton, CT: Morehouse-Barlow, 1982.

Wuthnow, Robert. *After Heaven: Spirituality in America Since the 1950s.* Berkeley: University of California Press, 2002.

Yates, Nigel. *Anglican Ritualism in Victorian Britain, 1830–1910.* Oxford: Oxford University Press, 1999.

Yollin, Patricia. "New Interest in Jewish Mysticism." *San Francisco Chronicle,* February 26, 2003.

Zaehner, R. C. *Mysticism Sacred and Profane: An Inquiry into some Varieties of Praeter-Natural Experience.* London: Oxford University Press, 1957.

INDEX

148 *Index*